Learning Language Arts Through Literature

THE YELLOW
TEACHER BOOK

By

Debbie Strayer

and

Susan Simpson

Common Sense Press

The *Learning Language Arts Through Literature* series:

The Blue Book - 1st Grade Skills
The Red Book - 2nd Grade Skills
The Yellow Book - 3rd Grade Skills
The Orange Book - 4th Grade Skills
The Purple Book - 5th Grade Skills
The Tan Book - 6th Grade Skills
The Green Book - 7th Grade Skills
The Gray Book - 8th Grade Skills
The Gold Book - *American Literature* - High School Skills
The Gold Book - *British Literature* - High School Skills

Copyright ©1998 by:
Common Sense Press, Inc.
8786 Highway 21
Melrose, FL 32666
www.commonsensepress.com

Printed in the United States of America.

Rev 06/08

ISBN 978-1-929683-22-2

Table of Contents

Materials to Use

To use this manual you will need pencils, paper, colored pencils, and drawing paper. Any additional materials are listed in the Teacher Notes at the beginning of each lesson.

Previous lessons are often used again, so keep all the student's work until the entire program is completed.

Reference books, such as a dictionary, thesaurus, and encyclopedia may be required.

Student Activity Books

Student Activity Books are available for your student. Daily exercises corresponding to each lesson are included for easy use. *Enrichment Activities* are also included.

The *Student Activity Book* is not a duplicate of the *Teacher Book,* therefore does not contain all the information found in the *Teacher Book.* The *Student Activity Book* is **not** intended for use without its companion *Teacher Book.*

Introduction

As parents we watched and marveled at the way our little ones learned to talk. By listening and responding to English spoken well, they were able to communicate quite clearly. The process was so gradual that they were not even aware it was taking place.

It is the belief of those associated with the *Learning Language Arts Through Literature* series that written language can best be learned in the same manner. By reading fine literature and working with good models of writing, children will receive a quality education in language arts. If you desire to teach using this integrated approach to language, this curriculum is for you.

Dr. Ruth Beechick has confirmed that this method of teaching is an appropriate and successful way to introduce our young students to the joys of reading, writing, and thinking. Our own experiences using these lessons with young children have encouraged us to share them with you. Their enjoyment and enthusiasm for reading and writing is an unmatched recommendation for this method of teaching.

The **integrated language approach** has the benefits of all teaching methods. By working with pieces of real literature, you focus on grammar, reading, vocabulary, spelling, writing, thinking skills, and penmanship. Your student has the best advantage for learning skills in this effective and lasting manner.

How to Use this Book

This book provides you with materials, activities, and suggestions that will encourage and benefit you as you create a learning environment for your student. Since everyone is different, we suggest that you try our ideas, and then freely experiment until you find patterns that work for you.

This manual is written in numbered lessons for easy reference. The easy-to-use format will make your teaching easier and more effective. A lesson usually takes about one week to complete, depending on you and your student.

Lessons contain a passage of literature and learning activities. These activities are designed to help your student learn language skills in their context while developing writing and thinking skills.

Grammar

Grammar is taught in conjunction with reading and writing, not as an isolated subject. An emphasis is placed on grammar skills appropriate for the third grade level. The student will either copy or write the literature passage from dictation. Copying material is a very powerful learning activity. It trains a student to look for details, strive for accuracy, and learn to write. After the student has made his first copy, ask him to check it with the model and make any necessary corrections. When dictation is used in the lesson, the passage will need to be read clearly, sentence by sentence. It is also important to use your voice to stress pauses and indicate punctuation marks.

Since this method may be new to you, here are a few suggestions:
1. Before dictation or copying, read the entire passage to your student.
2. Begin the dictation by reading one sentence at a time. If necessary, repeat the sentence, reading it one phrase at a time.
3. Instruct your student to leave a blank space between each line so that corrections are easy to make.
4. After dictation or copying, allow your student to use the passage to edit the work. At first, have the student check his work one line or phrase at a time. Asking the student to correct the work all at once may prove to be frustrating.

Reading Skills

Literature Links and **Comprehension Checks** throughout the program enhance your student's reading abilities. You may select the short stories included in the manual, or you may choose the following optional books:
The White Stallion by Elizabeth Shub
Madeline by Ludwig Bemelman
Meet George Washington by Joan Heilbroner
The Courage of Sarah Noble by Alice Dalgliesh

These books are written on a third grade readability level and will be enjoyed by all students. **Vocabulary** and discussion questions provide additional reinforcement of reading skills.

Spelling

Focus on Spelling is included in each lesson. Words have been carefully selected to help your student learn essential spelling tips that will provide him with the tools needed as he progresses in the series. Students are taught using the **See-Say-Spell** method. Encourage your student to look and see how the word is spelled, say the word aloud, and then spell the word. By using a multi-sensory method, your student has the advantage of seeing, saying, and spelling.

A spelling bee is given on Day 3. Ask your student to spell the words out loud. If he has problems, show him the word, then ask him to try again. Spelling tests at this level are optional.

Higher-Order Thinking Skills

Higher-Order Thinking Skills are developed throughout the activities in this manual. When your student is asked to respond to the literature with discussion, writing, drawing, or completing an activity, he is developing his thinking skills.

Creative Writing

Writing skills are developed within the context of learning reading and grammar skills. Your student is given ample opportunity to express ideas through drawing and writing. The beginning of creative writing is creative thinking. If your student is an apprehensive writer, allow him to dictate the sentences to you. He will be pleased with the sentences he has created and will eventually move into more independent writing.

Handwriting

As your student learns cursive writing, encourage him in his own ability. The handwriting illustrations in this manual show a realistic style. We recommend that you not compare his handwriting to a perfect model. He will improve as the year progresses and develops his own style as he matures.

Review Activities

New skills taught in each lesson are included in the *Review Activities* found directly after most of the lessons. It is not necessary to do each activity. Choose the skills your student needs.

Assessments

Assessments are included in the program for your use. An *I C.A.N. Assessment* has been created for each *Literature Link*. At this grade level you can expect your student to complete his work neatly with a good attitude. Use these assessments to evaluate your student's progress and assign a grade if needed.

Skills Index

The *Skills Index* is located in the back of the manual. To ensure that the language arts skills commonly held appropriate for third grade instruction were adequately covered, much research was involved in the writing of this book.

Bibliography

Next you will find the bibliography. This will give you all the information you need to locate the books quoted in the lessons. The selection includes wonderful books that we hope your family will read and enjoy.

Enrichment Activities

In each lesson you will find the treasure chest icon for the *Enrichment Activities*. This is your cue to look for the activity located in the *Student Activity Book*. Answers to these activities are found in this manual, page 285. While optional, these activities develop thinking and reasoning skills necessary for higher level learning.

EVERYDAY WORDS

New Skills

Base or Root Word	Synonym
Capitalization	Telling Sentences
Compound Words	Cause and Effect
Noun	Alphabetical Order
Period	Phone Book
Proper Noun	Thesaurus

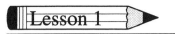

Teacher's Note:
As your student completes each lesson, choose skills from the *Review Activities* that he needs. The *Review Activities* follow each lesson.

Teacher's Note:
The spelling words consist of five words. The Bonus Word is optional.

See page 285.

We are glad God gave us the Bible. We call it God's Word because it tells us the things He wants us to know. God wants us to know that He made us. He wants us to know how to do what is right and how to worship Him.

Bible Stories to Read by Martha Rohrer.
Used by permission, Rod and Staff, Inc.
Crockett, Kentucky 41413.

1. a. Listen as your teacher reads the literature passage. Copy the sentences. Compare your copy to the literature passage and make corrections.

   b. Copy the spelling words from *Focus on Spelling*. Say the words aloud as you write them. Notice that these words spell the **/n/** sound with **kn**.

Focus on Spelling

knot   know   knife   knock   knee
Bonus Word: because

---

2. a. Listen as your teacher reads the following words:

   boy   girl   city   month   love

   These words are called **nouns** because they name a person, place, or thing.

Grammar Guide

Noun - person, place, thing, or idea

---

   b. Make a list of the people in your family. Make sure you begin each name (first and last name) with a capital letter. These words are called **proper nouns** because they name a specific person, place, or thing. Proper nouns always begin with a **capital letter**.

> ## Grammar Guide
>
> **Proper noun** - name of a particular person, place, or thing. Proper nouns are spelled with a capital letter.

c. Underline the words in our sentences that start with capital letters and are *not* at the beginning of a sentence.

d. Why do you think the words you underlined start with capital letters?

e. Discuss with your teacher what each underlined word means. Orally, make up a sentence using each word you underlined.

f. **SEE-SPELL-SAY:** Look and **see** each word on the spelling list. **Spell** each word aloud. **Say** the word.

3. a. Looking in the literature passage, find a word that begins with a silent letter and circle that word.

b. When the letters **kn** appear at the beginning of a word, what sound begins that word? **Kn** is a consonant pair where the **k** is silent.

> ## Phonics Fact
>
> **kn** at the beginning of a word says **/n/**

c. Look at this list of words. Say each word, remembering what sound **kn** makes.

knot   know   knew   knee   knife   knock

d. Cross out the **k** to show it is silent, like this: ̸knife.

2.
c. God, Bible, God's Word, He, Him

d. They refer to God and the Bible.

3.
a. know

b. /n/ sound

e. 1) knife
   2) know
   3) knee
   4) knock
   5) knot

✎ **Teacher's Note:**
Use this time as an oral review of your student's spelling words.

4.
a. period

✎ **Teacher's Note:** Telling sentences are called declarative sentences.

b. Begin the sentence with a capital letter, and end it with a period.

c. 1) My mother is going to the store.
   2) The car is red and very old.
   3) We get up at seven o'clock in the morning.
   4) The bears at the zoo look hungry.
   5) A big cat is sitting in the yard.

5.
a. God wants us to know that He made us. He wants us to know how to do what is right and how to worship Him.

e. Use the words to fill in the blanks for these sentences:

    knot   know   knee   knife   knock

1) Mom will cut the cake with a _____.
2) I _____ God loves me.
3) The boy fell off his bike and hurt his _____.
4) When the mailman brings my box, he will _____ on the door.
5) Dad will tie a _____ in the rope so we can swing on it.

f. Practice your spelling words in a Spelling Bee.

4. a. Look at the sentences in our literature passage. What punctuation mark is used at the end of each sentence?

b. The sentences in our literature passage are **telling sentences**. A telling sentence ends with a **period**.

Punctuation Pointer
Period - (.) ends a telling sentence

Two things are wrong with this telling sentence. Tell your teacher how to fix it.

      we are glad God gave us the Bible

c. Correct these either orally or in writing.
   1) my mother is going to the store
   2) the car is red and very old
   3) we get up at seven o'clock in the morning
   4) the bears at the zoo look hungry
   5) a big cat is sitting in the yard

d. Choose a book you like to read. Show your teacher at least two telling sentences.

e. Take your spelling pretest today.

5. a. Looking at the literature passage, read the sentences to your teacher that answer the question, "What does God want us to know?"

b. Write two or three sentences telling what you have learned from the Bible about what is right. Remember to begin each sentence with a capital letter and end with a period. Discuss your sentences with your teacher.

c. Optional: Take your spelling test today.

See page 285.

★

Handwriting

Student Activity Book Page 6

This year, you will be learning cursive writing. It may seem hard at first, but in a short time you will be writing sentences with no problems. Cursive writing is fun and helpful. You can write faster in cursive.

To write in cursive, remember three things:

1. Sit up straight, but comfortably, in your chair.
2. Place your writing paper on a slant.
3. Hold your pen or pencil correctly.

Teacher's Note:
Slant the writing paper accordingly for the left - handed student.

Teacher's Note:
The Common Sense Natural Handwriting System:

Much care, research and thought went into the development of *The Common Sense Natural Handwriting System.* We desired to present a system that gives students a basis for the formation of the letters, rather than a hard and fast template that they are forced to follow. We do understand that not all the letters are exactly alike. They were not meant to be. All of us, in reality, have some variation in the way we form letters, depending upon several factors, including other letters in the word we are writing.

We believe that *The Common Sense Natural Handwriting System* will benefit your students and instill in them a love for writing. As always, we welcome your comments, especially in the form of handwritten notes from your students.

1.
a. Tom
b. Nancy, Tampa
c. Maple Street,
   Lincoln Center

2.
a. We went to the zoo.
b. The doctor is late.
c. A big dog ran through
   our yard.
d. They will bring the cake.

Review Activities

Choose the skills your student needs to review.

1. *Proper Nouns*
   Circle all the proper nouns in the lists below.

a. Tom	boy	come	today
b. girl	Nancy	city	Tampa
c. building	Maple Street	Lincoln Center	church

2. *Capitalization and Punctuation*
   Rewrite each sentence, adding capitalization and punctuation.

   a. we went to the zoo
   b. the doctor is late
   c. a big dog ran through our yard
   d. they will bring the cake

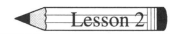

"Everything was safe and all right when Jesus was there. And it's still like that today," said Grandma. "If Jesus is with us, loving us and looking after us, then everything is safe and happy. But we have to ask him."

The Other Kitten by Patricia St. John.
Used by permission, 1984, Bethany House Publishers.

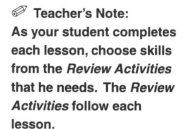

Teacher's Note: As your student completes each lesson, choose skills from the *Review Activities* that he needs. The *Review Activities* follow each lesson.

1. a. Listen as your teacher reads the literature passage. Copy the sentences. Compare your copy to the literature passage and make corrections.

   b. Copy the spelling words from *Focus on Spelling*. Say the words aloud as you write them.

> ## Focus on Spelling
> every everybody everyone everything everywhere
> **Bonus Word:** Grandma

Teacher's Note: The word *Grandma* in the literature passage is capitalized because it is used as a person's name.

Usually, words referring to God and the Bible are capitalized. However, the author has chosen to use a lower case *h* in *him* in this literature passage.

2. a. By reading the literature passage, we learn many of the things that Jesus does for us. Underline the words that tell how we feel when Jesus is with us.

   b. The underlined words are words that describe how we feel. The word *safe* is one of those words. The words *all right* means almost the same as *safe*. Words with the same or almost the same meaning are called **synonyms**.

> ### Grammar Guide
> **Synonym** - a word of similar meaning

★ ———————————————

See page 285.

2.
a. safe, all right

c. We are going to use a thesaurus with this activity.
A **thesaurus** is a collection of synonyms arranged in
alphabetical order like a dictionary. A thesaurus helps us
understand what words mean by telling us other words that
mean almost the same thing.

> ### Using Your Tools
>
> A **thesaurus** is a book of synonyms
> listed in alphabetical order.

2.

d. Answers may include huge, large, giant, grand, etc.

d. Practice using your thesaurus by looking up the word *big*.
Copy at least three synonyms for the word *big*. Using a
thesaurus, pick three words from our literature passage and
find a synonym, or a word with a close meaning, for each of
your words. Orally, make up a sentence using each word.
Try your synonym in its place. Did it mean the same thing?

e. **SEE-SPELL-SAY:**   Look and **see** each spelling word on the
spelling list. **Spell** each word aloud. **Say** the word.

3. a. The main part of a word is called the **base** or **root word.**
Look at this word: *helping*

The base word is *help*. An extra letter or letters added to the
end of a base word is called a **suffix**. The suffix in the word,
helping, is **-ing.**

b. Today, you will learn two ways to add the suffix **-ing** and **-ed**.
Read the *Grammar Guides*.

> ### Grammar Guide
>
> To add the suffix **-ing** or **-ed** to a word
> ending in silent **e**, first drop the **e**, and
> then add the suffix.
>
> Ex: bake - baking, baked

```
┌────────────────────────────────────────────┐
│              Grammar Guide                   │
├────────────────────────────────────────────┤
│  To add the suffix -ing or -ed to a         │
│  one-syllable word ending with a            │
│  short vowel and a consonant, double the    │
│  last consonant, and then add the suffix.   │
│                                             │
│  Ex:  stop - stopping, stopped              │
└────────────────────────────────────────────┘
```

c. Look at the literature passage. Find two words which end with the suffix **-ing**. Circle the words with a red pencil.

d. Add the suffixes **-ing** and **-ed** to the following words.
   Ex: bake   baking   baked   Ex: stop   stopping   stopped
   1) joke   5) jog
   2) care   6) pat
   3) hike   7) hop
   4) race   8) clap

e. Practice your spelling words in a Spelling Bee.

4. a. Sometimes two separate words can be put together to make a new word. This is called a **compound word**. Read these examples to your teacher.

   out + side = outside   side + walk = sidewalk
   base + ball = baseball   cup + cake = cupcake

```
┌────────────────────────────────────────────┐
│              Grammar Guide                   │
├────────────────────────────────────────────┤
│  Compound Word - two words                  │
│  joined together to make a new word         │
└────────────────────────────────────────────┘
```

b. There are three different compound words in our literature passage. Find them and underline them with a colored pencil. Draw a line between the two words that have been joined together.

✎ **Teacher's Note:** Your student may pick out the word *everything*. Just show him that in this case, the *-ing* is part of the word, not a suffix.

3.
c. loving, looking

d. 1) joking   joked
    2) caring   cared
    3) hiking   hiked
    4) racing   raced
    5) jogging   jogged
    6) patting   patted
    7) hopping   hopped
    8) clapping   clapped

4.
b. every/thing, to/day, Grand/ma

c. mail/man   every/where
    foot/ball   bed/room
    birth/day

d. 1) birthday
    2) football
    3) everywhere
    4) mailman
    5) bedroom

See page 285.

c. Read this list of compound words to your teacher. Draw a line between the two words that have been joined together.

    mailman everywhere football bedroom birthday

d. Orally or in writing, use the list of compound words you just divided to complete these sentences.
    1) I will be nine years old on my _____.
    2) My father and I like to play _____.
    3) We looked _____ for our lost dog.
    4) The _____ puts letters in the box by the road.
    5) My _____ is a good place to play and sleep.

e. Take your oral or written spelling pretest today.

5. a. Listen as your teacher reads the story from Matthew 14:22-33 of Jesus walking on the water. On a separate piece of paper, draw pictures showing the disciples before and after Jesus came. How can this story help you when you are afraid?

b. Optional: Take your spelling test today.

★

    o o

    d d

    a

    c

Review Activities

Choose the skills your student needs to review.

1. *Synonym*
   Write a synonym for each word.

   a. big
   b. little
   c. safe
   d. fluffy

2. *Suffix -ing*
   Add the suffix **-ing** to these words.

   a. take
   b. win
   c. run
   d. care
   e. bite
   f. stop

3. *Compound Word*
   Circle the compound words.

   mailman
   enough
   everywhere
   bedroom
   birthday
   water

---

1. Possible answers.
a. **large, huge**
b. **small, tiny**
c. **secure, protected**
d. **fuzzy, furry**

2.
a. **taking**
b. **winning**
c. **running**
d. **caring**
e. **biting**
f. **stopping**

3.
mailman
everywhere
bedroom
birthday

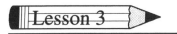
✎ **Teacher's Note:**
As your student completes each lesson, choose skills from the *Review Activities* that he needs. The *Review Activities* follow each lesson.

✎ **Teacher's Note:**
Inform your student the pronoun *he* in the literature passage refers to a boy named Mark.

See page 285.

2.

a. Compound words are two words joined together to make a new word.

b. Grandma, lighthouse, herself, shopkeeper

c. Possible answers include flashlight, sunlight, doghouse, housewife, myself, himself.

See page 285.

For the first time he started to feel really worried, not just about Grandma and the lighthouse, but about Carol herself. He went back to the shop but the shopkeeper hadn't seen her.

The Other Kitten by Patricia St. John.
Used by permission.©1984. Bethany House Publishers.

1. a. Listen as your teacher reads the literature passage. Copy the sentences from the model. Compare your copy to the literature passage and make corrections.

   b. Copy the spelling words from *Focus on Spelling*. Say the words aloud as you write them. Notice that these words spell the /ē/ sound with **ee**.

   > ## Focus on Spelling
   > *feel   keep   wheel   seen   need*
   > **Bonus Word:** *really*

2. a. In Lesson 2, you learned about compound words. Tell your teacher what compound words are, reviewing that activity if necessary.

   b. Find the compound words in our literature passage and underline them.

   c. Can you think of any other compound words that include these words? (The words may be used as the first or second part of the word.)

   > light   house   self

   d. Use the compound words from your list in either oral or written sentences.

   e. **SEE-SPELL-SAY:** Look and **see** each spelling word on the spelling list. **Spell** each word aloud. **Say** the word.

3. a. The suffix, or ending, **-ed** has been added to two words in the literature passage. Find these words and underline them.

b. In Lesson 2, you learned two ways to add the suffixes **-ing** and **-ed**. Today, you will learn another way to add the suffix **-ed** to words ending with a consonant **y**. Read the *Grammar Guide*.

> ### Grammar Guide
>
> When adding the suffix **- ed** to words ending in a consonant and **y**, first change the **y** to **i**, and then add **-ed**.
>
> Ex: worry - worried

Add the suffix **- ed** to the following words.
Ex: worry worried

1) try
2) hurry
3) carry
4) empty

c. Use the words you have made in **3c** to fill in these blanks:

1) Dad _____ the bags into the house.
2) Mom said we were late, so we all _____ to get dressed.
3) The wheel kept falling off my wagon, so I _____ to fix it.
4) The trash was full, so my brother _____ it.

d. Practice your spelling words in a Spelling Bee.

4. a. In Lesson 2, your teacher read you the Bible story found in Matthew 14:22-33. We learned about some events that took place and their outcome. The events that took place are the **cause**. The outcome of these events is the **effect**. There are several of these elements in our story. One of the effects was that the water and storm were quieted. What do you think was the cause?

Remind your student that the pronoun *he* in the literature passage refers to Mark.

4.
b. Mark is worried because he cannot find Carol.

c. Possible answers:
1) He or she was hurt.
2) They went on vacation.
3) Someone has been cooking.
4) Someone went shopping.

d. Answers will vary.

b. In our literature passage, we see that Mark is very worried. This is an effect. Though we have not read it directly, what do you think caused Mark's worry?

c. There are examples of cause and effect in our daily lives. Listen to these effects, and think of possible causes:

1) Your sister or brother is crying.
2) My mother and father are very happy.
3) There is a warm meal on the table.
4) You have a new shirt or dress to wear.

d. Talking with your teacher, think of an event, person, or feeling that made you worry. Write at least three sentences telling about this situation. In the fourth sentence tell how the situation turned out. Remember to begin your sentence with a capital letter and end it with a period.

e. Take an oral or written spelling pretest.

5. a. Listen to your teacher as she reads the vocabulary words to you.

Vocabulary			
seashore	different	sea gulls	castle
wonderful	animals	wind	enough
smooth	shovel	quiet	listen

b. Read the story, "The Seashore," to your teacher.

✏ Teacher's Note:
Help your student with any needed pronunciation during the reading.

The Seashore

The seashore is a wonderful place to visit where you can find neat things to look at and fun things to do. Many seashores have sand where the water meets the land which is called a beach. Some beaches have sand that is soft and fun to play in. If you have a shovel, you can dig a hole or build a castle in the sand.

The sea comes up to the shore in waves. Sometimes, the wind makes the waves very big, and other times, the waves are smooth and quiet. If it is warm enough, people swim in the sea. Some people like to float if the waves are not too rough.

Many different things live at the seashore. Fish are found in the sea water. Some animals swim in the water. Other animals, like crabs, crawl on the sand. Some animals, like seagulls, can walk on the sand, float in the water, or fly in the air. There always seems to be something moving at the seashore.

When you come to the seashore, look for pretty shells. Try to catch a wave as it comes up on the sand. Listen to birds call to each other and dive for fish. Then you can tell your own seashore story.

c. Discussion Questions

1) What is the sandy place called where the water meets the land?
2) What can you do in the sand?
3) What kind of animals live at the seashore?

d. Optional: Take your spelling test today.

5.
b. 1) The Beach
   2) You can dig a hole, build a sand castle, and do many other things.
   3) There are fish in the water, crabs in the water and on land, sea gulls in the air and many other creatures.

See page 285.

★

i   i

t   t

a   c

o

d   d

Review Activities

Choose the skills your student needs to review.

1. *Suffix -ed*
   Add the suffix **-ed** to the following words.

   a. worry
   b. carry
   c. bury
   d. empty

   1.
   a. worried
   b. carried
   c. buried
   d. emptied

2. *Proper Nouns*
   Circle the proper nouns.

   Lucy   house   store
   dog   Food Mart   Aunt Sally

   2. Lucy, Food Mart,
   Aunt Sally

3. *Capitalization and Punctuation*
   Rewrite each sentence, adding capitalization and punctuation.

   a. the car is clean now
   b. that cat is pretty
   c. we went to the store

   3.
   a. The car is clean now.
   b. That cat is pretty.
   c. We went to the store.

4. *Suffix -ing*
   Add the suffix **-ing** to these words.

   a. hop
   b. stop
   c. fake
   d. move

   4.
   a. hopping
   b. stopping
   c. faking
   d. moving

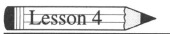

✎ Teacher's Note:
As your student completes each lesson, choose skills from the *Review Activities* that he needs. The *Review Activities* follow each lesson.

He looked up at her and saw that her eyes were shut like when she prayed at night, and he knew that she was praying for Carol.

The Other Kitten by Patricia St. John.
Used by permission, 1984,
Bethany House Publishers.

1. a. Listen as your teacher reads the literature passage. Copy the sentence. Compare your copy to the literature passage and make corrections.

   b. Copy the spelling words from *Focus on Spelling*. Say the words aloud as you write them. Notice that these words spell the /ā/ sound with **ay**.

Focus on Spelling

pray   crayon   holiday   gray   stay
Bonus Word: *were*

See page 285. ⎯⎯⎯⎯⎯⎯⎯⎯⎯⎯⎯⎯ ★

2.
a. night

b. ni̶g̶ht

2. a. One of the words in our literature passage has two letters in the middle of the word that are silent. Circle the word.

   b. What sounds do you hear in the word *night*? Cross out the two silent letters in the word *night*. When the letters **gh** follow **i**, they are silent, and **i** says /ī/.

   Phonics Fact

   When **gh** follows **i**, the **gh** is silent, and **i** says /ī/.

c. Possible answers include light, sight, fright, might, fight.

   c. Make as many words as you can by adding one or two letters to the beginning of these letters: _____ight
   Ex: bright

   Show your teacher and read the words to her.

18

d. Read the following list of words to your teacher.

flight   night   fight   slight   right

Use the words above to complete the following sentences:

1) He writes with his _____ hand.
2) If you don't stop them, the dog and cat will _____.
3) The boy fell from a low chair, so his bump is _____.
4) The stars are pretty at _____.
5) Our _____ to Grandma's house leaves at ten o'clock.

e. **SEE-SPELL-SAY:** Look and **see** each word on the spelling list. **Spell** each word aloud. **Say** the word.

3. a. In Lesson 1, **2b,** we introduced proper nouns. Review the *Grammar Guide* in Lesson 1. Proper nouns are the names of particular people, places, or things. They begin with capital letters. Tell your teacher the proper nouns in these sentences:

1) Bob lives in a big house in New York.
2) My brother Jack is in town.
3) He likes to go to Disney World.

b. Look back at the literature passages for Lessons 2, 3, and 4. Make a list of the proper nouns used in these lessons.

c. Make up three sentences using the following proper nouns:
1) a particular person's name
2) a particular place's name
3) a particular thing's name

d. Practice your spelling words in a Spelling Bee.

2.
d. 1) right
   2) fight
   3) slight
   4) night
   5) flight

3.
a. 1) Bob, New York
   2) Jack
   3) Disney World

b. Lesson 2 - Jesus, Grandma
   Lesson 3 - Grandma, Carol
   Lesson 4 - Carol

See page 285.

4. a. In Lessons 2 and 3, you learned about adding suffixes to the ends of words. Review these *Grammar Guides*.

Today, you will learn how to add **-ing** to words ending in **y**. Read the following *Grammar Guide*.

> ## Grammar Guide
>
> To add the suffix **- ing** to words ending in **y**, just add **- ing**.
>
> Ex: play - playing   worry - worrying

b. Add the suffix **-ing** to the end of these words.
Ex: play   playing

1) say
2) pay
3) stay
4) pray

5) try
6) hurry
7) carry
8) empty

c. You have learned four ways to add a suffix to the end of a word. Today, you will learn the last one. Read the *Grammar Guide*.

> ## Grammar Guide
>
> When adding the suffix **-ed** and **-ing** to all other words, just add the suffix.
>
> Ex: help - helped - helping
>   leak - leaked - leaking

d. Add **-ed** and **-ing** to the end of these words.
Ex: help   helped   helping

1) ask
2) need
3) wash
4) peel
5) paint
6) call

4.
b. 1) saying   5) trying
   2) paying   6) hurrying
   3) staying   7) carrying
   4) praying   8) emptying

d. 1) asked   asking
   2) needed   needing
   3) washed   washing
   4) peeled   peeling
   5) painted   painting
   6) called   calling

e. You have a list of eight words with suffixes from **4b**. Use some of these words to complete these sentences:

1) Mary is _____ for her sick uncle.
2) The men are _____ heavy boxes.
3) My aunt is _____ with us.
4) I am _____ to learn to ride a bike.
5) My neighbor is _____ me to walk his dog.

f. Take your oral or written spelling pretest today.

5. a. How would you feel if you were Mark? Your sister seems to be lost, and you may feel like it's your fault. What if you were Carol? What if you were Grandma? Pretend you are each person, and tell how you think you would feel. To know more about what happens, you may want to read the whole story.

b. In the literature passage from Lesson 2, Grandma told Mark and Carol how Jesus takes care of us. How do we ask Jesus to take care of us? Discuss this with your teacher.

c. Prayer is the way we talk to God. The Lord's Prayer is an example of a prayer. (Read it in Matthew 6:9-13.) Is there something you need Jesus to take care of? Write down a prayer, asking Jesus for that help.

d. Some people keep a journal or notebook in which they write down the things they pray about. Talk with your teacher about this. See if you can write down one thing each day that you have prayed about. In a few weeks, look back on your list and notice any answers that have been given to your prayers. You may want to put a star by these items or color them with a highlighting marker.

e. Optional: Take your spelling test today.

★ ———————————

e. 1) praying
2) carrying
3) staying
4) trying
5) paying

5.
b. Prayer

See page 285.

e   e

l   l

a   c

o   d

i   t

Review Activities

1. *Suffix **-ing***
   Add the suffix **-ing** to these words ending in **y**.

   a. stay
   b. carry
   c. try
   d. say

2. *Suffix **-ing** and **-ed***
   Add the suffix **-ing** and **-ed** to these words.

	-ing	**-ed**
a. ask		
b. yell		
c. talk		
d. peel		

3. *Compound Words*
   Circle the compound words

mailman	everyone	carpenter
today	someone	doctor

1.
a. staying
b. carrying
c. trying
d. saying

2.

	-ing	-ed
a.	asking	asked
b.	yelling	yelled
c.	talking	talked
d.	peeling	peeled

3.
mailman
everyone
today
someone

23

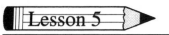

Here is a section of a make-believe phone book:

Automobiles
Al's Fast Cars - 23 Big Street - 341-2190
Sam's Slow Cars - 14 Little Street -755-1011

Bakeries
Betty's Better Bread - 12 Butter Road -368-4392
Peachy Pies - 75 Sweet Tooth Lane - 983-0555

Camps
Happy Camper Cabins - Happy Valley - 225-3232

✏ **Teacher's Note:**
As your student completes each lesson, choose skills from the *Review Activities* that he needs. The *Review Activities* follow each lesson.

✏ **Teacher's Note:**
Your student will need a local phone book.

See page 286.

2.
a. Name of the business, address, phone number

b. 1) Al's Fast Cars, Sam's Slow Cars
2) Peachy Pies
3) Happy Camper Cabins
4) Betty's Better Bread

See page 286.

3.
a. Yellow Pages or business listings

1.   Listen as your teacher reads the listings. Copy the bolded section of the business listings leaving a blank line between each entry. Compare your copy to the model and make corrections.

2. a. Reading our make-believe phone book can give you much information. Discuss with your teacher the information each listing gives.

   b. Listen as your teacher reads the following sentences. Tell her the name of a business in our phone book that might be able to help.

     1) Bob wants to buy a new car.
     2) Mom needs a dessert for a party.
     3) Your family wants to go on vacation.
     4) Grandma needs to make sandwiches for a picnic.

3. a. The entries that we read in our make-believe phone book are from a certain part of the phone book. Looking at your local phone book, see if you can find the same part of your phone book.

b. The listings are also in a certain order. What do you think this order is called?

If we needed to add another bakery, such as *Carol's Cookies, 55 Apple Avenue, 818-3774*, where would we put it?
Please add this to your listings in the proper place.

c. Not only are the topics (automobiles, bakeries, camps) in alphabetical order but also the businesses themselves. Using your local phone book, find two listings for bakeries and automobiles. Look at your copy of the phone listings. Decide where each listing should appear, and copy it in the correct place.

Choose a topic that you want to know about, and look it up in the phone book. On a separate piece of paper, copy a listing for that topic as well.

4. a. Your friend needs to find a plumber to fix his water pipes. Orally, decide what steps he should take.

b. Now, by yourself or with your teacher as your secretary, make a written list of the steps your friend needs to take to fix his water pipes. Start with getting a phone book and end with waving goodbye to the plumber. Make sure to number your list and to put a period after each number.

c. Read your list out loud. Do the steps make sense? Did you forget anything? Ask your teacher's opinion on this.

d. Review the spelling words from Lessons 1-4.

 ———————————————————

5. a. Either orally or in writing, spell the following words for your teacher.

1)	knee	I fell and hurt my *knee*.
2)	every	*Every* seat in the car was taken.
3)	wheel	The bike needs a new *wheel*.
4)	pray	Before we go to bed, we *pray*.
5)	knock	Open the door when you hear a *knock*.
6)	need	I *need* to eat.
7)	holiday	Thanksgiving is a *holiday*.
8)	everywhere	Mary took her lamb *everywhere*.

b. Alphabetical order

***Carol's Cookies* goes between *Betty's Better Bread* and *Peachy Pies*.**

4.
a. Posssible Answers: Get a phone book, look up *plumbers*, call the plumber, have the plumber come to the house, watch the plumber work, pay the plumber, and wave goodbye.

b. Possible Answers:
1) **Get a phone book.**
2) **Look up *plumbers*.**
3) **Call the plumber.**
4) **Have the plumber come to the house.**
5) **Watch the plumber work.**
6) **Pay the plumber.**
7) **Wave good-bye to the plumber.**

See page 286.

5.
a. ✐ Teacher's Note: You may give sentences if your student needs it to understand the word given.

b. ✐ **Teacher's Note: Read the sentence to your student to be written from dictation. Read slowly, repeating it several times. Encourage your student to just listen the first time, and then begin. Do not be concerned about saying it too often. The goal is for your student to be able to write the sentence. Speed and accuracy will be increased over time.**

c. ✐ **Teacher's Note: After your student's first attempt, show him how to correct any mistakes. Read the sentence again, several times if needed. Repeat the correction process. Make sure to praise improvements. He may attempt it a third time if he desires; however, be alert to fatigue. If your student is overly tired or discouraged at this point, it is best to end the session, highlighting improvements.**

b. Listen to your teacher as she dictates a sentence to you.

Everybody will need a holiday.

c. After your teacher has checked your sentence, make any corrections.

Cover your paper so that you can not see your corrected sentence. Listen again to your teacher as she dictates the same sentence again. Repeat the correction process.

u   u

s   s

o   d

i   t

e   l

Review Activities

1. *Using the phone book*

   Use the phone book listing at the beginning of Lesson 5 to answer these questions.

   a. Where would you call to order pies for a party?
      What is the phone number?

   b. Where would you call if you wanted to take a camping vacation?
      What is the phone number?

   c. Which car lot is on Little Street?
      What is the phone number?

1.
a. **Peachy Pies 983-0555**
b. **Happy Camper Cabins**
   225-3232
c. **Sam's Slow Cars**
   755-1011

Assessment 1
(Lessons 1 - 5)

1. Rewrite these sentences, adding capitalization and punctuation.

   a. she was late for the party
   b. he went to the store
   c. we like cake

2. Circle the proper nouns.

   girl   boy   Tom   dog   Main Street

3. Write a synonym for each word.

   a. big
   b. little

4. Adding the suffix **-ing** to these words.

   a. give
   b. win
   c. move
   d. stay
   e. try
   f. hop

5. Add the suffix **-ed** to these words.

   a. carry
   b. clean
   c. bury

6. Make two compound words using the word *every*.

1.
a. She was late for the party.
b. He went to the store.
c. We like cake.

2.
a. Tom
   Main Street

3. Possible answers:
a. huge, large
b. tiny, small

4.
a. giving
b. winning
c. moving
d. staying
e. trying
f. hopping

5.
a. carried
b. cleaned
c. buried

6. Possible answers:
   everyone
   everyday
   everything

Literature Link

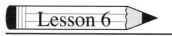

Literature Link

1. There are two options for this week's lesson.

The White Stallion
by Elizabeth Shub
Published by
Random House

Option 1 - Find the book, *The White Stallion* by Elizabeth Shub, from the library and read half of the story today.

Summary
The White Stallion

This story is a retelling of a story passed from generation to generation. The beginning of the book says it is a true story. During the early 1800's, many families moved to the West. The family of a girl named Gretchen was one of those families. While on their trip out west, Gretchen accidentally becomes separated from her family while riding the family horse, Anna. Anna follows a herd of wild mustangs and meets up with a big white stallion. The mustangs begin to nibble at the cornmeal tied to Anna's back, and they nip Gretchen, too. The big white stallion does an amazing thing, and Gretchen is left alone by the horses. After a long and lonely night, the herd returns, much to Gretchen's delight. The stallion again behaves in a most unusual way, and Anna and Gretchen return to the camp.

✎ **Teacher's Note:**
Remind student of any needed pronunciation during reading.

Option 2 - Listen to the vocabulary words as your teacher reads them to you. Read half the story of "Tilda the Troublemaker."

Vocabulary			
Tilda	Tennessee	troublemaker	chicken
visitors	special	invited	outwit
enough	bridle	saddle	reins
different	comfortable		

Tilda the Troublemaker

As a little girl, going to my grandpa's farm was the best trip. Mom, Dad, and I would drive to Grandpa's little town. We would leave on Friday, and it would take hours to get there. Riding in the car was fun because we ate chicken out of a box. Sometimes, my mom would play games with me while we drove. Sometimes, I would read or draw to pass the time; sometimes, I would sleep. Finally, we would get to the small town where my grandpa lived.

My grandpa's old farm was always a special place for me. He had lived there for many years. Grandma and Grandpa were always happy to see us, and they invited us to the best tasting dinners I ever ate. Chickens and cows were there, as were the pecan and pear trees. All the things on the farm seemed wonderful. The one thing that was best though was Tilda.

Tilda was a Tennessee Walking Horse. This was funny because she didn't like to do much walking. A better name for her would have been a Tennessee Resting Horse. She had lived there ever since the first time I visited Grandpa's old farm. Tilda had been Grandpa's horse for a long time. She was a warm dark brown with a black tail and mane. Her face had a smart look to it, as if she were trying to outwit the people around her. She had a white blaze on her head that made her look pretty.

If you came to see Tilda, it was best to bring food — and lots of it. She would lift her head to look at visitors, and then she would come if you held out your hand as if you had a snack. We would bring sugar cubes, which were her favorite, and carrots. Mom showed me how to feed her so I wouldn't get a bite from her big teeth. (Carrots and fingers can look alike.)

The best part of visiting Tilda was getting to ride her. While it was best for me, it was not something she liked to do. If you weren't quick, like Grandpa, Tilda would run away when she saw the bridle. Grandpa would call her to come. They seemed to fuss at each other, until the bridle was on. She would wait while he saddled her without too much fussing. I found that a sugar cube every now and then helped. Then she would be ready to ride.

Mom, Dad, or Grandpa would ride her first because sometimes she would show her temper. After that, I would get to ride her. I had to hang on to the saddle horn. The world looked very different from Tilda's back. She seemed so tall, and I felt very tall as well. Until I was nine or so, someone always held the reins while I rode. Then I got to hold the reins sometimes but only for Tilda to walk around the farmyard.

Tilda was a very smart horse. She would think of ways to get a rider off her back. One time, my dad was riding her in the pine forest. Tilda decided enough was enough. She turned and came trotting back to the barn. My dad talked to her and pulled on the reins, but Tilda didn't listen. Her sights were set on the barn. Soon he had a very big problem. Tilda was tall, and my dad was taller sitting on her. The barn door was much shorter than they were. Watching Tilda running into the barn with my dad ducking and yelling was a funny sight. I think even Tilda was laughing!

After a few years, I got to ride Tilda around the farm by myself. She was getting older, but she didn't seem to be any fonder of riding. One day, I was riding her in the pine forest. Well, do you know what happened? She decided she had had enough riding, and off to the barn she went. She ran very closely to the trees to bump my legs. I stayed in the saddle. Then she tried a new trick on me. She ran towards a fence and jumped over it. I was so busy holding on that I don't remember much, but when we got back to the barn, I started to fuss at her.

As I stood looking at her, she snorted and stamped her foot. She seemed to be telling me what I already knew. She and Grandpa had an understanding. The two of them had been together for a long time. Tilda felt comfortable with Grandpa on her back. She only let us ride her because we fed her sugar and carrots. I still think that Tilda liked going for those rides with the rest of us. She just had to tell us when enough was enough. To me, she was a troublemaker. She was also the best horse ever.

2. a. Finish reading the book or story from yesterday.

b. Discuss the following questions with your teacher.

Discussion Questions for *The White Stallion*:

1) How many families are in the wagon train? Who is in Gretchen's family that is traveling West?

2) Who is Anna? Why did Father tie Gretchen to Anna's back?

3) When did Father and Mother discover that Gretchen was missing? What did they do then?

4) How do you think the family felt during the night? How did Gretchen feel?

5) Tell how the wild horses acted friendly to Anna. What did the horses do that frightened Gretchen?

6) What amazing thing did the white stallion do? Do you think he was trying to help Gretchen?

7) What did Mother tell her to do if she were ever lost? Did she obey Mother?

8) How did Gretchen get back to her family? Do you think the white stallion helped again?

---

2. b. *The White Stallion*

a. 1) There are three families in the wagon train. Mother and Father, Trudy, John, Billy, and Gretchen.

2) Anna is the old family mare. She has two sacks of cornmeal tied to her back.

3) After the wagon he was fixed and the family was ready to eat, the family realized that Gretchen and Anna were missing. The men tried to follow the mare's tracks, but it was too dark.

4) The family probably felt very worried about little Gretchen. Gretchen did not realize that she was so far away from the wagon train. She was not afraid because the horses were so friendly.

5) The horses nuzzled and rubbed up against her.

Gretchen began to be afraid when the mares started to eat the cornmeal tied to Anna. They wanted the grain so much that they accidentally nibbled Gretchen's leg.

Answers continued on next page.

2.

b. 6) The white stallion bit through the ropes that tied Gretchen to Anna. Then he slowly lifted her off Anna and set her on the ground. He may have been trying to help Gretchen, or he may have been trying to help Anna.

7) Gretchen's mother told her, "If you are lost, stay where you are. That will make it easier to find you." She obeyed her mother.

8) Anna carried Gretchen back to her family. It seems that the white stallion was trying to help Gretchen get back to her family.

2.

b. "Tilda the Troublemaker"
1) Child, Mother and Father are traveling to Grandpa's.

Mother, Dad, Child, Grandpa

2) Tilda is a Tennessee Walking Horse. The name does not seem to fit her because she does not like to walk very much.

3) She liked the snacks they brought her. Her favorite snacks were sugar cubes and carrots.

4) She liked to ride Tilda the best.

5) stubborn

Discussion Questions for "Tilda the Troublemaker":

1) Who is traveling to Grandpa's farm? Make a list of the people mentioned in the first paragraph.

2) Who is Tilda? Does the name of her kind of horse seem to fit her? Tell why or why not.

3) What did Tilda like best about visitors? Name her favorite snacks.

4) What did the little girl in the story like best about visiting Tilda?

5) Choose the word that best describes Tilda's temperament, or attitude:

calm   mean   stubborn

6) Tell some of the ways Tilda would try to get riders off her back.

7) Tilda would let some people ride her, and then she would get tired of it and decide to go back to the barn. What phrase in the story best describes Tilda getting to this point? (Paragraphs 6 and 8)

8) How do you think the little girl really feels about Tilda?

c. Look up these words in a dictionary and develop your vocabulary on horses. You may just read them, or you may read them and write them down.

mustang	mare	stallion
colt	whinny	neigh
nuzzle	nip	herd

3. a. Storytelling was often the only way history was passed from one generation to the next. Ask your parents if there are any stories told in your family that have been passed from one generation to the next. It might be something funny or exciting that happened to your relatives years ago. Try to remember the story and retell it.

b. Here are some pictures of horses. Orally or in writing, describe the horses in the pictures to your teacher. Use as many adjectives, or describing words, as you can. Here is an example: The big dark horse has a beautiful long mane.

6) She would run very close to trees to try to rub her rider off. She would run under things too low for her rider to fit under, like a barn doorway. She also jumped over a fence.

7) "She decided she had had enough of riding, and off to the barn she went."

8) If you don't know, read the last line of the story. She thinks Tilda was the best horse ever.

4. a. Here is a chart that shows the parts of a horse. Read the names of the parts to your teacher. You may want to color the horse or trace your own horse picture by placing white paper over the chart.

mane

muzzle

tail

flank

hoof

4.
b. 1) mane
 2) hoof
 3) tail
 4) muzzle
 5) flanks

b. Fill in the sentence blanks with the correct parts.
   mane   muzzle   flanks   hoof   tail

1) The hair on the horse's neck is called his _____.
2) Often a horseshoe is put on a horse's _____.
3) On summer days, a horse will use his long _____ to swish away flies.
4) The horse's nose and _____are very soft and sensitive.
5) The horse's strong _____ help him run fast and work hard.

5. a. To finish your study on horses, tell your teacher about the horse you would like to have. You may use the following suggested questions:

1) What would you name your horse?
2) What would he or she look like (remember to use the names of the horse parts and adjectives to describe your horse)?
3) What would you do with your horse?
4) How would you feel about your horse?

b. After answering these questions, write a sentence to answer
    each question. (For example, "I will name my horse Flash.")
    After deciding what you will write, make your final copy.

c. A group of sentences which tells about one main idea is
    called a paragraph. Begin your paragraph by indenting
    (bringing in from the left margin about one inch) your first
    sentence.

> ### Focus on Writing
> A **paragraph** is a group of sentences
> that tell about one **main idea**. **Indent**
> the first sentence of a paragraph.

d. To complete your horse story, you may want to draw a picture
    that includes what you think your horse would look like.
    Share your story and picture with someone.

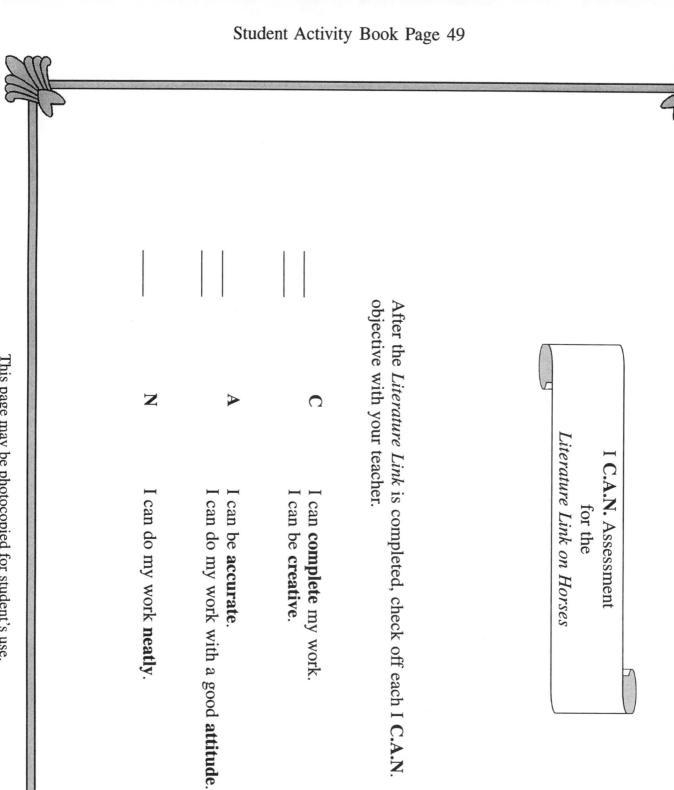

I C.A.N. Assessment
for the
Literature Link on Horses

After the *Literature Link* is completed, check off each I C.A.N.
objective with your teacher.

C	I can **complete** my work.
	I can be **creative**.
A	I can be **accurate**.
	I can do my work with a good **attitude**.
N	I can do my work **neatly**.

EVERYDAY WORDS

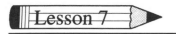

Teacher's Note:
As your student completes each lesson, choose skills from the *Review Activities* that he needs. The *Review Activities* follow each lesson.

Teacher's Note:
Tell your student that in poetry, sometimes each line begins with a capital letter even if it doesn't begin a new sentence.

See page 286.

I want to learn to whistle.
I've always wanted to.
I fix my mouth to do it but
The whistle won't come through.

"Whistles" by Dorothy Aldis reprinted by permission of G.P. Putnam's Sons from *Here, There, and Everywhere* by Dorothy Aldis, copyright 1927, 1928, copyright renewed 1955, 1956 by Dorothy Aldis.

1. a. Listen as your teacher reads the poem. Copy the poem. Compare your copy to the literature passage and make corrections.

   b. Copy the spelling words from *Focus on Spelling*. Say the words aloud as you write them. Notice that these words spell the **/oo/** and **/ow/** sound with **ou**.

   > ### Focus on Spelling
   > through group mouth count ground
   > **Bonus Word:** always

2. a. **Contractions** are shortened words that are made by joining two words together with an **apostrophe** (') to show that a letter(s) has been taken out.

   > **Grammar Guide**
   >
   > **Contractions** - two words joined together with an apostrophe to replace missing letter(s)

   > **Punctuation Pointer**
   >
   > **Apostrophe** - (') replaces missing letter(s) in a contraction

Read these words to your teacher, and write the words that make up the contractions. Tell your teacher which letters have been removed and replaced by an apostrophe:

1) isn't   3) I'll
2) wasn't   4) I'm

b. There are two contractions in the literature passage. Find them and underline them. What words were combined to make these contractions?

c. Here is a list of commonly used contractions. Make up sentences orally using each contraction.

I + have = I've   I + will = I'll
can + not = can't   do + not = don't
will + not = won't   is + not = isn't
did + not = didn't   are + not = aren't

d. Underline the contraction in each sentence. Either orally or in writing, repeat the sentence, taking out the contraction and replacing it with the two words that make up the contraction.

1) I'll have more cake.
2) Dad can't find his hammer.
3) The book isn't on the table.
4) Mom didn't fix dinner tonight.
5) We aren't ready for winter.
6) We don't need to get a new car.

e. Is it easier to say the sentences with or without the contractions? Which do you think is easier to understand?

f. **SEE-SPELL-SAY:** Look and **see** each spelling word on the list. **Spell** each word aloud. **Say** the word.

3. a. The word *whistle* ends in the letters **-le**. Read the following words to your teacher, and tell what sound **-le** makes.

table   people   paddle   turtle   waffle   gurgle

2.
a. 1) is not   o
   2) was not   o
   3) I will   wi
   4) I am   a

b. I've - I have
   won't - will not

c. ✎ Teacher's Note:
   The contraction *won't* is different from most contractions because the spelling of the word *will* changes.

d. 1) I'll - I will
   2) can't - can not
   3) isn't - is not
   4) didn't - did not
   5) aren't - are not
   6) don't - do not

e. Answers will vary.

3.
a. -le says /l/

43

3.

b. ta/ble, peo/ple,
pad/dle, tur/tle,
waf/fle, gur/gle

✎ **Teacher's Note: Words
ending in** *ckle* **are divided
like this: chuck/le**

**c. 1) paddle
2) waffle
3) people
4) table
5) turtle
6) gurgle**

See page 286.

b. Words are made up of sounds. A single uninterrupted sound
is called a **syllable**. When you have a word with a consonant
followed by **-le** at the end of a word, those letters plus the
consonant before it usually make up one syllable.
Ex: ruf/fle

Divide the list of words from **3a** into syllables by drawing a
line between the two syllables.

Phonics Fact

The letters **-le** at the end of a word
will usually form its own syllable
with the consonant before it.

---

c. Use the list of words from **3a** to fill in these sentence blanks.

1) While crossing the lake in the boat, he lost the _____.
2) I had eggs and a _____ for breakfast.
3) Many _____ came to the party.
4) Please come and set the _____.
5) The green _____ swam around the lake.
6) The water made a sound like a _____.

d. Practice your spelling words in a Spelling Bee.

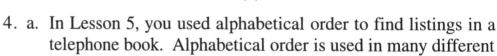 ★

4. a. In Lesson 5, you used alphabetical order to find listings in a
telephone book. Alphabetical order is used in many different
ways. Together with your teacher, make a list of the first
names of six friends. Rewrite the names in alphabetical
order.

b. Look at this pattern: *Smith, Ann*

This is often the way names are written, with the last name
first and then the first name. Write your name following this
pattern.

c. Rewrite your list, following the pattern of last name first, then a
comma, then first name, in alphabetical order by the last names.

d. Did the order of the names change from when you used first names? Where would your name fit on this list?

e. Take your oral or written spelling pretest today.

★ ───────────────────────────────

See page 286.

5. a. The poem in our literature passage describes an activity many people can do — whistle. Is whistling difficult for you? Do you remember when you first learned to whistle? Discuss with your teacher the experience of whistling or learning to whistle.

b. Whistling is an activity that people can do for different reasons. Make a list of the reasons people might whistle. The items on the list do not have to be complete sentences. Number your list, and put a period after each number.

5.
b. Possible answers:
   to call a dog, for fun,
   to make a musical tune,
   to get someone's
   attention, etc.

c. This verse tells about wanting to be able to do something, yet not being able to do it. Write a paragraph of three or four sentences telling about something you want to do but can't. Please include how you feel about it. Everyone has things he can't do. Remember to capitalize the first word of every sentence and end with a period. Indent the first sentence of the paragraph.

d. Optional: Take your spelling test today.

★ ───────────────────────────────

See page 286.

m   m

n   n

i   t

e   l

w   s

Review Activities

1. *Contractions*
   List the two words that make up the contractions.

   a. isn't
   b. don't
   c. can't
   d. I'll

2. *Syllables*
   Divide the words into syllables.

   a. table
   b. turtle
   c. little
   d. paddle

3. *Alphabetical order*
   List the names in alphabetical order.

   Emily
   Ann
   Dan
   Tom

1.
a. is not
b. do not
c. can not
d. I will

2.
a. ta/ble
b. tur/tle
c. lit/tle
d. pad/dle

3.
Ann
Dan
Emily
Tom

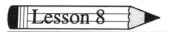
✐ **Teacher's Note:**
As your student completes each lesson, choose skills from the *Review Activities* that he needs. The *Review Activities* follow each lesson.

See page 286.

2.
a. swallow

✐ **Teacher's Note:**
Whistle and *can* may also be nouns or verbs.

b. - a type of bird
    - to pass from the mouth
     to the stomach

✐ **Teacher's Note:**
Some grammar books refer to these words as homographs.

c. *bank* - ground bordering a lake or river or a place for keeping and issuing money
duck - a swimming bird or to lower your head to avoid something
bat - a flying mammal or what you use to play baseball
top - a spinning toy or opposite of bottom

I think perhaps it's stuck, and so
I try it once again.
Can people swallow whistles?
Where is my whistle then?

"Whistles" by Dorothy Aldis reprinted by permission of G.P. Putnam's Sons from *Here, There and Everywhere* by Dorothy Aldis, copyright 1927, 1928, copyright renewed 1955, 1956 by Dorothy Aldis.

1. a. Listen as your teacher reads the poem. Copy the sentences. Compare your copy to the literature passage and make corrections.

   b. Copy the spelling words from *Focus on Spelling*. Say the words aloud as you write them. Notice that the /ō/ sound at the end of each word is spelled **ow**.

Focus on Spelling
yellow   swallow   follow   pillow   shadow
Bonus Word: *perhaps*

★

2. a. Sometimes a word can have more than one meaning. Can you find a word in your verse that is both an object and an action?

   b. The word *swallow* has more than one meaning. Look up this word in the dictionary and write two definitions (or meanings) for it. Words that sound the same, have different meanings, and are sometimes spelled the same are called **homonyms**.

   c. Here are some other words that have more than one meaning. Read the homonyms to your teacher, and tell her the meanings you know for each word. Look up the words in a dictionary if you can't think of more than one meaning for them.

     bank   duck   bat   top

d. Use the words from **2c** to fill in these sentence blanks.

   1) When we need money, we go to the _____.
   2) The _____ is swimming in the water.
   3) The park is on the _____ of the river.
   4) If you are tall, sometimes you have to _____ your head.
   5) The boy watched the _____ spin around.
   6) She hit the ball with the _____.
   7) I climbed to the _____ of the ladder.
   8) I saw a _____ flying into a cave.

e. **SEE-SPELL-SAY:** Look and **see** each word on the spelling list. **Spell** each word aloud. **Say** the word.

3. a. Contractions are shortened ways of writing words. Two words have been put together to make a new word. Letters are usually taken out and replaced by an apostrophe ('). There is a contraction in our literature passage. Find it, and underline it. What two words do you think went together to make this contraction?

   b. Here is how you make this contraction: it + is = it's. Read this list of words, and tell your teacher how you think these contractions should be spelled:

      1) he + is   4) I + am
      2) she + is   5) we + are
      3) you + are   6) they + are

   c. Rewrite the sentences below and replace the words in italics with a contraction made in **3b**.

      Remember to start each sentence with a capital letter.

      1) *She is* going to the park.
      2) *They are* waiting for the bus.
      3) *I am* fixing dinner.
      4) *We are* driving to Grandma's house.
      5) *You are* not the last one in line.
      6) *He is* running to first base.

2.
d. 1) bank
   2) duck
   3) bank
   4) duck
   5) top
   6) bat
   7) top
   8) bat

3.
a. it's
   it is

b. 1) he's
   2) she's
   3) you're
   4) I'm
   5) we're
   6) they're

c. 1) She's
   2) They're
   3) I'm
   4) We're
   5) You're
   6) He's

See page 286.

4.
a. perhaps

✐ **Teacher's Note:**
**A thesaurus is needed
for this activity. A junior
thesaurus would be
easiest for your student
to use.**

c. Possible answers
  **1) huge, enormous,
     gigantic**
  2) ran, trotted, galloped
  **3) great, marvelous,
     delicious**
  **4) called, shouted,
     announced**

See page 286.

5.
a. "I try it once again."

---

d. Look in a favorite book, and find some contractions. Make a list of at least five contractions. Show the list to your teacher, and tell her what words were put together to make each contraction.

e. Practice spelling words in a Spelling Bee.

4. a. When we write or speak, we often use the same words over and over. One word that we can use too often is the word *maybe*. In our verse there is a word that means the same as *maybe*. This word is a synonym, or a word close in meaning, to the word *maybe*. Underline the word.

b. Try using the word *perhaps* in place of the word *maybe* for a couple of days. You may be surprised by how often you say *maybe*.

c. Look at a thesaurus with your teacher. A thesaurus is a collection of synonyms, or words that are close in meaning to other words.

Look up the following words in a thesaurus, and choose two synonyms for each word. Remember, the thesaurus is arranged in alphabetical order like a dictionary.

1) big   2) went   3) good   4) said

d. Either orally or in writing, use one of your synonyms to replace the words in italics.

1) The horse *went* back to the barn.
2) This birthday cake tastes *good*.
3) Mother *said*, "It is time to come in."
4) The *big* dog jumped into the car.

e. Take your oral or written spelling pretest today.

5. a. When we want to be able to do something and can't, sometimes we give up. Is that what this person has done? Read the line in the verse to your teacher that answers this question.

b. Think of something that you kept trying to do, and then were able to do. Did you give up trying? Draw a picture or write several sentences that show how practice helped you.

c. Think about the sentences you wrote in our last lesson describing something you couldn't do. Would practice help you be able to do it? Discuss this with your teacher.

d. Can you think of stories about people or characters who wanted to do something but had a hard time? With practice, or by continuing to try, they were able to accomplish their goal. Talk with your teacher about any of these familiar stories:

   1) The tortoise in "The Tortoise and the Hare" (Aesop's Fables)
   2) The engine in "The Little Engine That Could" (Watty Piper)
   3) The crow in "The Crow and the Pitcher" (Aesop's Fables)

e. Optional: Take your spelling test today.

Review Activities

1. *Synonyms*
Give two meanings for each word.

   a. bank
   b. bat

2. *Contractions*
Write the contraction for each of these words.

   a. do not
   b. it is
   c. you are
   d. we are
   e. she is
   f. I am

3. *Synonyms*
Rewrite the sentences, replacing the underlined words with a synonym.

   a. This sandwich is good.
   b. The little kitten climbed on me.
   c. We went to the fair.

1.
a. a place where money is kept; the land by a river

b. a small flying mammal; a wooden stick used to hit a ball

2.
a. don't
b. it's
c. you're
d. we're
e. she's
f. I'm

3. Possible answers:
a. fine, delicious
b. small, tiny
c. walked, wandered

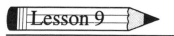

August 20, 1998

Dear Grandma and Grandpa,

    How are you? We are all fine.
We went to the beach today.
It was fun. Billy and I found some
small shells. It was very hot.
Please come to see us soon.

           Love,
           Ann

Teacher's Note:
As your student completes each lesson, choose skills from the *Review Activities* that he needs. The *Review Activities* follow each lesson.

1. a. Listen as your teacher reads the letter. Copy the letter. Compare your copy and make corrections.

   b. Copy the spelling words from *Focus on Spelling*. Say the words aloud as you write them. Notice that these words spell the /ē/ sound with **ea**.

   > ## Focus on Spelling
   > beach   treat   clean   peace   leave
   > **Bonus Word:** sincerely

See page 286.

2.
a. It is written to a friend.

2. a. This is an example of a **friendly letter**. There are five parts to a friendly letter: **heading**, **greeting**, **body**, **closing**, and **signature**. Why do you think it is called a friendly letter?

> ## Focus on Writing
> A **friendly letter** consists of a heading, greeting, body, closing, and signature.

b. red - August 20, 1998
  blue - Dear Grandma and Grandpa,
  yellow - box around body of letter (all of the sentences)
  green - Love,
  orange - Ann

   b. Using different colored pencils or crayons, find and underline each part of the letter as it is named:
   red - heading (or date)
   blue - greeting (or saying hello)
   yellow - draw a box around the body of the letter
   green - closing (or saying goodbye)
   orange - signature (or name of person writing the letter)

c. Now that you have named the different parts of a friendly letter, discuss with your teacher where we use capital letters and commas when writing a friendly letter.

Capital letters are used to start all parts of the letter and in all names in the greeting. Commas are used after the day in the date, after the greeting, and after the closing.

d. Ask your teacher if she has a friendly letter she has received. With her permission, use your colored pencils on the letter. Mark the letter the same way we did in **2b**.

e. **SEE-SPELL-SAY:**   Look and **see** each word on the spelling list. **Spell** each word aloud. **Say** the word.

3. a. In our letter, there are two places where the word *and* is used with names. Circle the word *and*. This is called a **conjunction**, a word used to join words or sentences.

```
┌─────────────────────────────┐
│      Grammar Guide          │
├─────────────────────────────┤
│  Conjunction - a word that  │
│  joins words or sentences   │
└─────────────────────────────┘
```

b. When we see the conjunction *and* we know that two parts have been connected. What naming words were connected by the word *and*?

c. Say the name of a family member and then yourself, remembering to name yourself last.

_____ and _____ tickle each other.

(name of family member)   *(yourself)*

Do we use the word *me* to name ourselves? What word do we use? When you are talking about someone and yourself, always name yourself last.

3.
b. Grandma, Grandpa;
Billy, I

c. Ex: Dad and I tickle each other.
No
I

d. 1) Sue and Ann can play.

2) Mom and I will cook dinner.

3) Dan and Jon went camping.

4) Grandma and Grandpa can hug me.

5) Jack and I found a kitten.

See page 286. ──────

d. Make some new sentences by using the conjunction *and*.
   Ex: Bob went swimming. + Bill went swimming. =
         Bob and Bill went swimming.

   1) Sue can play. + Ann can play. =
   2) Mom will cook dinner. + I will cook dinner. =
   3) Dan went camping. + Jon went camping. =
   4) Grandma can hug me. + Grandpa can hug me. =
   5) Jack found a kitten. + I found a kitten. =

e. Practice your spelling words in a Spelling Bee.

4. a. Now it is your turn to write a friendly letter. Choose someone who would like a letter from you. Talk with your teacher about what you want to say in the body, or message of the letter.

   b. Follow the form in our letter, making sure you have five parts: heading, greeting, body, closing, and signature.

   c. When you have finished your letter, look at the envelope below. Follow the format when addressing your envelope.

   Jerry Brown
   10 Red Road
   Anywhere, CA 90000

               stamp

                    Mary Jones
                    123 Fun Street
                    Somewhere, FL 30000

   ---

   d. With your teacher's permission, place your letter in the envelope and seal it. Place a stamp in the upper right hand corner and mail it. Now you can look forward to getting a reply.

   e. Take your oral or written spelling pretest today.

See page 287. ──────

5. a. One of the best ways to check comprehension, or understanding, is to follow directions. In this activity, you are to read the directions on the following pages, and follow them to make a paper airplane. With your teacher, first read the "Glossary of Words and Symbols" so you will know how to follow the directions. Remember to follow directions exactly so your airplane will fly!

Extra Activity: Make your own design for a paper airplane, telling your teacher how to do each step along the way. When you are finished, ask someone to try to make your airplane by following the directions you gave. Were they clear enough? Did you leave out any steps?

   b. Optional: Take your spelling test today.

★ ———————————————

✐ **Teacher's Note:**
For more ideas on paper airplanes, find *The Easy to Make Paper Airplane Book* **by Lane Simpson, published by Common Sense Press.**

See page 285.

Glossary of Words and Symbols

─────────────	Shows the sides of the paper
— — — — — — —	Shows where the fold is to be made
▪ ▪ ▪ ▪ ▪ ▪ ▪ ▪ ▪ ▪ ▪	Shows a crease made from a previous fold
⤷	Shows the direction the fold is to be made
a, b, c, d, X's	Letters are used to help in the direction
long ways	Fold to make the center fold down the longest part of the paper

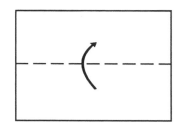

short ways	Fold to make the center fold down the shortest part of the paper

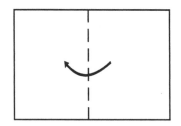

thumbcrease	To fold paper over with your thumb. The fold is the size of your thumb and used on back of wings.
notebook paper	Standard 3 hole notebook paper or plain copy or computer paper

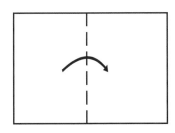

1. Fold paper in half short ways. Open paper.

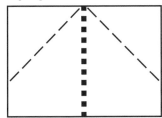

2. Fold corners to meet at the middle fold.

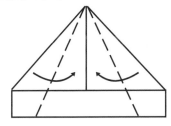

3. Fold sides over again to meet at middle fold (will overlap at bottom).

4. Fold wings back at dotted lines — wings overlap body at each side.

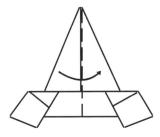

5. Fold plane in half — line up wings and crease fold.

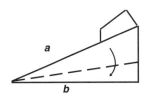

6. Fold down wing at dotted line — match side **a** with side **b** — on both sides.

7. Folding wing sides up.

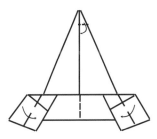

8. Fold nose of plane back into center fold. Press sides together at tip to hold it in place.

<u>Flying Instruction:</u>

Hold in middle of fuselage — holding the plane up a little bit, throw gently.

Review Activities

1. *Friendly Letter*
   Label the parts of a friendly letter:
   signature   greeting   date   body   closing

                                    July 10, 1998

                              a. _____

   Dear Sally,

   b. _____

      Hello.   I hope you are having a fun vacation.
   I can hardly wait for you to come back.

         c. _____

            Love,

            d. _____

            Sue

            e. _____

---

2. *Conjunctions*
   Rewrite the two sentences by using a conjunction to
   make one sentence.

   a. Nancy can run. Joe can run.
   b. Dad fixed the car. I fixed the car.

1.
a. date
b. greeting
c. body
d. closing
e. signature

2.
a. Nancy and Joe
   can run.
b. Dad and I fixed the car.

61

1.
a. don't
b. we're
c. I'll
d. you'll
e. can't
f. I'm

2.
a. rid/dle
b. cir/cle
c. tur/tle
d. sum/mer

3.
Dan
Joe
Mike
Zack

4. Possible answers
a. fluffy
b. large

5.
a. Tom and Dan went fishing.
b. Lucy and Emily had fun.

Assessment 2
(Lessons 7 - 9)

1. Write the contractions for these words.
   a. do not
   b. we are
   c. I will
   d. you will
   e. can not
   f. I am

2. Divide these words into syllables.
   a. riddle
   b. circle
   c. turtle
   d. summer

3. List these names in alphabetical order.
   Joe Dan Zack Mike

4. Rewrite the sentences by replacing the underlined words with synonyms.

   a. This pillow is <u>soft</u>.
   b. We like <u>big</u> dogs.

5. Rewrite the two sentences by using a conjunction to make one sentence.

   a. Tom went fishing. Dan went fishing.
   b. Lucy had fun. Emily had fun.

Raining, raining,
All night long;
Sometimes loud, sometimes soft,
Just like a song.

"Rain in the Night"
by Amelia Josephine Burr

1. a. Listen as your teacher reads the poem. Write the lines from dictation the second time she reads them, or copy them. Compare your copy to the poem and make corrections.

   b. Copy the spelling words from *Focus on Spelling*. Say the words aloud as you write them. Notice that the Bonus Word spells the /ī/ sound with **igh**.

Focus on Spelling

some somebody something sometimes somewhere
Bonus Word: night

★ ———————————————————————

2. a. Find the word *raining* in your poem. Underline the letters **r-a-i-n**. This is the main part of the word called the base or root word. The word *rain* is a doing word called a verb.

> **Grammar Guide**
> **Verb** - a doing word

   b. Sometimes extra letters are added to the end of a word. This is called a suffix. Circle the suffix added to the word *raining*.

   c. When we add the suffix **-ing** to the end of a doing word or verb, we show that the action of the word is continuing to happen. From our sentence, how do we know that the rain is continuing?

✐ **Teacher's Note:**
If you choose to dictate, tell your student when to begin a new line. Also, tell him that in this poem, the first word in each line is capitalized.

See page 287.

✐ **Teacher's Note:**
The word *rain* may also be used as a noun.

2.
b. - ing

c. The poem says, "Raining, raining, all night long"

63

2.
d. 1) laughing
   2) growing
   3) holding
   4) falling
   5) drinking
   6) cleaning

e. 1) cleaning
   2) growing
   3) holding
   4) laughing
   5) drinking
   6) falling

3.
a. loud, soft

b. 1) sometimes
   2) night
   3) long
   4) all

d. Add the suffix **-ing** to these doing words, or verbs, and pantomime, or act them out, for others to guess:

1) laugh + ing   3) hold + ing   5) drink + ing
2) grow + ing   4) fall + ing   6) clean + ing

e. Use the words you made in **2c** to fill in the following blanks:

1) We are _____ the house.
2) The flowers in the garden are _____.
3) My mother is _____the baby.
4) I was _____at the clowns.
5) The bird was _____from the bird bath.
6) The rain has been _____all day.

f. **SEE-SPELL-SAY:** Look and **see** each spelling word on the spelling list. **Spell** each word aloud. **Say** the word.

3. a. When we hear words that are the opposite of one another, it helps us understand how different things can be. A word of opposite meaning is called an **antonym**.

> **Grammar Guide**
>
> **Antonym** - a word of opposite meaning

In the poem, find the two words that are opposites, or antonyms, and underline them with a red pencil or crayon.

b. There are other words in our poem for which we can think of an opposite, or antonym. Look at the poem as your teacher reads these words. Find the antonym in the poem for each word she reads:

1) always   2) day   3) short   4) none

c. The following sentences don't make sense. Read each
sentence, and choose an opposite word from the list below
that needs to be used in place of the italicized word.

bright   small   loud   sweet   long

1) The ringing alarm was *quiet.*
2) The ant is a very *big* bug.
3) The sugar is very *sour.*
4) The sun is very *dark* during the day.
5) The *short* snake was lying across the road.

d. Talking with your teacher, make up a list of words that are
opposites. Try to think of at least ten pairs of words that are
antonyms. Write each word on an index card. You should
have twenty cards. Shuffle the cards, and place them face
down in five rows of four cards each. Take turns turning over
two cards at a time, trying to match the antonyms. If you
make a match, you get another turn. Continue until all the
pairs are matched. To make the game more challenging, you
may add more antonym pairs.

e. Practice your spelling words in a Spelling Bee.

——————————————

4. a. The vowel that comes before the consonant pair **-ng** usually
makes its short sound. There are several words in our
literature passage that end with the consonant pair **-ng**.
Find and circle each one.

> ### Phonics Fact
> The vowel before **-ng** usually
> says its short sound.

b. Look at this list of words. Underline the **-ng** ending in each
word.

long	king	rang
song	string	sang
strong	bring	bang
along	thing	clang

3.

c. 1) The ringing alarm was
loud.

    2) The ant is a very *small*
bug.

    3) The sugar is very
sweet.

    4) The sun is very *bright*
during the day.

    5) The *long* snake was
lying across the road.

2.

d. ✎ **Teacher's Note:**
Help your student in
spelling these words.

See page 287.

4.
a. raining, long, song

4.

**c. They make their short
   vowel sound.**

d. 1) string
   2) rang
   3) along
   4) king
   5) strong
   6) bang

See page 287.

5.
Possible Answers
b. 1) She is happy.
   2) He looks angry.
   3) The student is busy.

c. What vowel sound do the vowels make that come right before the letters **-ng**? Read the list of words in **4b** to your teacher.

d. Choose words from the list in **4b** to fill in the blanks to rhyme with the underlined words.

   1) The kite we will <u>bring</u> is on the end of a _____.
   2) We heard the bell <u>clang</u> when the fire alarm _____.
   3) When you learn the <u>song</u>, we can all sing ____.
   4) The golden, shiny <u>thing</u> sits on the head of a _____.
   5) The rope holding the boat was <u>long</u>, and it was also_____.
   6) We listened as the birds <u>sang</u>, and then we heard a gun go _____.

e. Take your oral or written spelling pretest today.

5. a. Have you ever listened to the rain? Discuss with your teacher the sounds you hear when it rains, and what those sounds remind you of. For example, rain on a tin roof can sound like a drum.

b. Different kinds of weather can describe different kinds of feelings. Talk with your teacher about these expressions. Try to tell your teacher, or show her by acting or drawing, what you think these expressions mean:

   1) She is feeling very sunny.
   2) His face looks stormy.
   3) That student is like a whirlwind.

c. Talk with your teacher and make up three sentences telling what you see, hear, and feel when it rains. Begin your paragraph by indenting the first sentence. Write a fourth sentence telling what you think about rain. Remember to begin your sentences with a capital letter and end with a period.

d. On a separate piece of paper, draw a picture to go with your sentences, describing your sentences. If you don't want to draw, try to find pictures in a magazine that show rain.

e. Optional: Take your spelling test today.

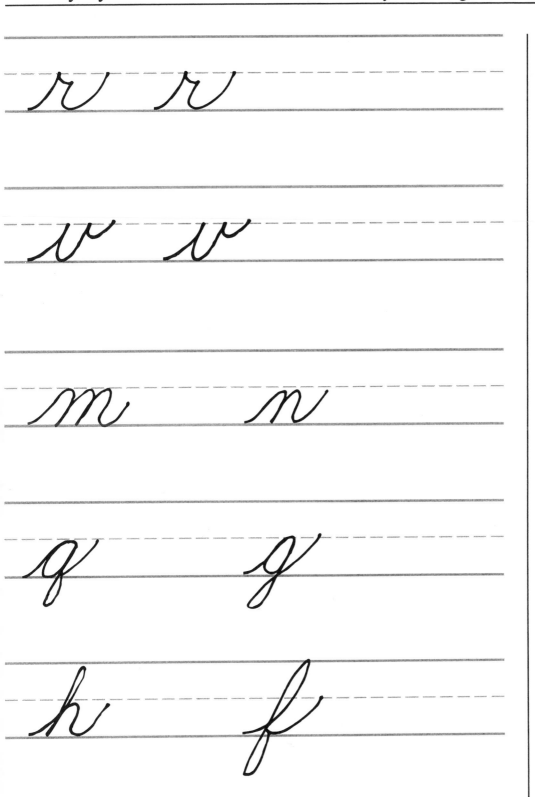

Review Activities

1.
a. grow
b. laughed
c. played
d. rained

2. Possible answers
a. quiet
b. dark
c. short
d. some

1. *Verbs*
   Circle the verb in each sentence.

   a. Our plants grow every day.
   b. I laughed at his jokes.
   c. Sam played with the kitten.
   d. It rained all night.

2. *Antonyms*
   Write an antonym for each word.

   a. loud
   b. light
   c. tall
   d. none

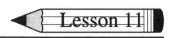

There'll be rivers in the gutters
And lakes along the street.
It will make our lazy kitty
Wash his little, dirty feet.

"Rain in the Night"
by Amelia Josephine Burr

✎ **Teacher's Note:**
As your student completes each lesson, choose skills from the *Review Activities* that he needs. The *Review Activities* follow each lesson.

1. a. Listen as your teacher reads the poem. Write the poem from dictation the second time she reads them, or copy it. Compare your copy to the model, and make corrections.

   b. Copy the spelling words from *Focus on Spelling*. Say the words aloud as you write them. Notice that these words spell the **/er/** sound with **ir**.

✎ **Teacher's Note: If you choose to dictate, tell your student when to begin a new line. Also, tell him that in this poem, the first word in each line is capitalized.**

> ### Focus on Spelling
> dirty   third   girl   bird   first
> **Bonus Word:** along

 ────────────────────

See page 288.

2. a. Describing words help us understand more about the people, places, or things (nouns) they talk about. Adjectives are words that describe people, places, or things.

> ### Grammar Guide
> **Adjective** - a word that describes a person, place, or thing

Underline in red the word that tells about or describes the noun, *kitty*.

   b. Our sentence says that the kitty is *lazy*. *Lazy* is an adjective which describes the kitty. Now, with a blue pencil, underline the words that tell about the kitty's feet.

2.
a. lazy

b. little, dirty

69

2.

c. Possible Answers
 1) **lazy dog**
    lazy day
 2) **little mouse**
    little bicycle
 3) **dirty floor**
    dirty shirt

d. 1) slow
 2) **sleepy**
 3) **soft**
 4) **big**
 5) **rainy**
 6) **happy**

3.
a. gutters, kitty, little

c. Using the three adjectives from our poem (*lazy, little, dirty*), think of nouns you can describe with these words. Remember, a noun names a person, place, or thing.

Make a list of at least two nouns that can go with each adjective:

1) lazy_____   2) little_____   3) dirty_____
   lazy_____   little_____   dirty_____

d. The kitty's feet are *little* and *dirty*. These describing words give us a fuller picture of the kitty. Read the following phrases to your teacher. Either orally or in writing, point out the adjective in each phrase:

1) a slow boat   3) a soft pillow   5) a rainy day
2) the sleepy dog   4) the big house   6) the happy baby

e. Can you imagine what this kitty looks like and acts like? Describe, draw, or act out what you think this kitty might be like.

f. **SEE-SPELL-SAY:** Look and **see** each spelling word on the spelling list. **Spell** each word aloud. **Say** the word.

3. a. When you want to know how many **syllables**, or parts, there are in a word, we have certain rules to go by. When double consonant letters are in the middle of a word, divide the word into syllables between the double consonant. Circle the words in your sentences that have two of the same consonant letters in the middle.

Phonics Fact

Syllable - part of a word which has a single vowel sound

---

b. One of the words in our poem with double consonant letters in the middle of the word is *kitty*. The word *kitty* has two syllables, or spoken parts. Say this word out loud. Do you hear the two parts (kit-ty)? As you say a word, you can clap each time you hear a syllable. Say *kitty* again, and clap for each part. Clap and say each of these words. Tell your teacher how many syllables you hear in each:

1) summer   4) little   7) happy
2) hello   5) dinner   8) better
3) middle   6) gutter   9) bigger

c. When there are two of the same consonant letters in the middle of a word, we divide the word between those two letters, like this: fun/ny. Divide the words you read in **3a**.

d. Practice your spelling words in a Spelling Bee.

★ ───────────────────────────

4. a. Read the following clues. Write the correct word in each blank. The answers are found in the previous literature passages:
   1) I want to learn to _____. (Lesson 7)
   2) ... he knew that she was _____for Carol. (Lesson 4)
   3) Dear Grandma and _____, (Lesson 9)
   4) Raining, _____, All night long; (Lesson 10)
   5) Can people _____whistles? (Lesson 8)
   6) There'll be _____in the gutters. (Lesson 11)
   7) _____was safe and all right. (Lesson 2)

b. Use the words you listed in **4a** to complete this crossword puzzle.

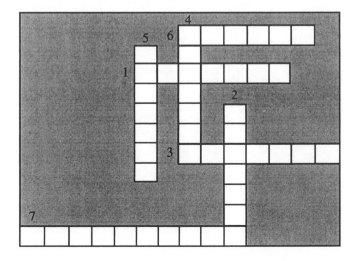

b. 2 syllables in each word.
1) sum/mer
2) hel/lo
3) mid/dle
4) lit/tle
5) din/ner
6) gut/ter
7) hap/py
8) bet/ter
9) big/ger

c. gut/ters kit/ty lit/tle

See page 288.

4.
a. 1) whistle
2) praying
3) Grandpa
4) raining
5) swallow
6) rivers
7) Everything

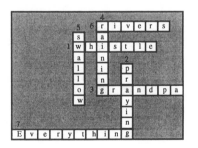

See page 288.

5.

b. The words rivers, *lakes*, and *gutters* makes one picture a heavy downpour.

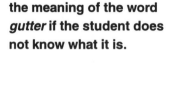 **Teacher's Note: Discuss the meaning of the word *gutter* if the student does not know what it is.**

See page 288.

c. Take your oral or written spelling pretest today.

★

5. a. Look up the words *river* and *lake* in the dictionary. Discuss the meanings with your teacher. Write the words and their meanings as you understand them.

b. As we read our sentences, we read that there will be *rivers* in the gutters and *lakes* along the streets. Do you think there are really going to be lakes and rivers in the street? Discuss with your teacher what picture the author is trying to paint by using these words.

c. Presenting a poem to other people can be fun. Begin to memorize the first and second verses of this poem (Lessons 10 and 11). You can memorize by reading the lines out loud until you can remember them. Practice saying these verses for others, so it will become easy for you to make a presentation. You may want to make a picture, or illustration, to use for each verse. (You can use your drawing from Lesson 10, **5d** for the first verse.)

d. Optional: Take your spelling test today.

★

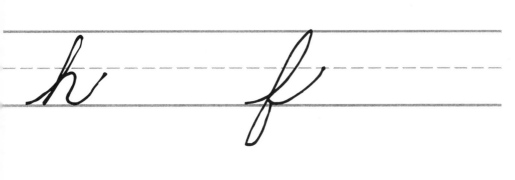

Review Activities

1.
a. lazy
b. little
c. dirty
d. soft

2.
a. hap/py
b. din/ner
c. mid/dle
d. pud/dle

1. *Adjectives*
   Circle the adjectives in the phrases.

   a. the lazy dog
   b. the little child
   c. the dirty cat
   d. the soft bed

2. *Syllables*
   Divide the words into syllables.

   a. happy
   b. dinner
   c. middle
   d. puddle

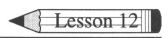

The roses will wear diamonds
Like kings and queens at court;
But the pansies all get muddy
Because they are so short.

"Rain in the Night"
by Amelia Josephine Burr

1. a. Listen as your teacher reads the poem. Write this poem from dictation the second time she reads it, or copy it. Compare your copy to the poem and make corrections.

   b. Copy the spelling words from *Focus on Spelling*. Say the words aloud as you write them. Notice that these words spell the /ā/ and /ē/ sound with **ea**.

   ### Focus on Spelling

   wear   year   clear   hear   dear
   Bonus Word: queen

 ————————————————————

2. a. There are several naming words, or nouns, in our poem that name more than one of each thing. For example, the word *kings* means more than one king. Underline each of the nouns, or naming words, that name more than one.

   b. How did we make each naming word mean more than one? What letter did we add to the end?

   c. The word *pansies* is a little different. One of these flowers is called a *pansy*. This is the **singular** form, meaning single or one. When you make a word mean more than one, it is called **plural**.

   ### Grammar Guide

   Singular - one
   Plural - more than one

   Look at this word, and tell how we changed it to mean more than one or plural.

   pansy - pansies

See page 288.

Teacher's Note:
As your student completes each lesson, choose skills from the *Review Activities* that he needs. The *Review Activities* follow each lesson.

Teacher's Note:
**If you choose to dictate, tell your student when to begin a new line.
Also, tell him that in this poem, the first word in each line is capitalized.**

2.
a. roses, diamonds, kings, queens, pansies

b. An s was added.

Teacher's Note:
When a word ends with a consonant and y, change the y to i before adding the plural ending -es.

c. When a word ends with a consonant and y, change the y to i and add -es. This changes the word from being one, which is singular, to being more than one, which is plural.

d. 1) bodies
   2) babies
   3) ponies
   4) candies
   5) copies
   6) jellies

3.
a. mud/dy

b. 1) slip/per
   2) run/ner
   3) bat/ter
   4) swim/mer
   5) hap/pen
   6) let/ter

c. 1) peo/ple
   2) rus/tle
   3) bee/tle
   4) trou/ble
   5) cir/cle
   6) cra/dle

See page 288.

d. Change these words to mean more than one:
   1) body 2) baby 3) pony 4) candy 5) copy 6) jelly

e. **SEE-SPELL-SAY:** Look and **see** each word on the spelling list. **Spell** each word aloud. **Say** the word.

3. a. You have learned about dividing words into syllables in Lessons 7 and 11. Syllables are the sounds that make up a word. Find the word in our literature passage that has double consonant letters in the middle of the word. Underline the word, and then draw a line to divide this word into two syllables.

  b. As you learned in Lesson 11, when there are double consonant letters in the middle of the word, you divide the word into syllables between the middle consonants.
   Ex: bet/ter

   Divide these words into syllables:
   1) slipper   4) swimmer
   2) runner   5) happen
   3) batter   6) letter

  c. As you learned in Lesson 7, when a word ends with a consonant and **-le**, you usually divide the word before the consonant which comes before **-le.**
   Ex: whis/tle.

   Divide these words into syllables:
   1) people   4) trouble
   2) rustle   5) circle
   3) beetle   6) cradle

  d. Practice your spelling words in a Spelling Bee.

4. a. In the literature passage we have two pictures; one of the roses and the other of the pansies. Discuss with your teacher what you think the author is telling you about each flower and how it fares in the rain.

> **Using Your Tools**
>
> The **encyclopedia** is a book or set of books that contains information on various topics.

b. Look up the names of the following flowers in an encyclopedia or a book about flowers, so you can see what they look like:

tulip   rose   pansy   sunflower   daisy

c. Write sentences describing each flower. Remember to use many describing words (adjectives) to tell about the color, size, and shape of each flower.

d. Include a picture or illustration of the flowers. You may draw these pictures or cut them out of magazines or seed catalogs.

e. Take your spelling pretest today.

★ ─────────────────────────────

5. a. To make our meaning more clear when we write, we sometimes use a simile (sĭm´ ĭ lē). A simile is a way of comparing two things by using the word *like*.
Ex: The rain sounded like drum beats.

Find the simile in our literature passage.

b. Read these similes, and try to imagine how they might look:
clouds that look like cotton balls
raindrops that shine like jewels
a kite that flies like a bird
flowers that smell like perfume

You may draw pictures that go with these similes.

4.

a. Possible answer:
   The rose bush is tall,
   so the raindrops will
   look like diamonds.
   The pansies are low to
   the ground, so the rain
   will make it muddy.

See page 288.

5.

a. The roses will wear
   diamonds *like* kings and
   queens at court

77

c. 1) frogs, jumping beans, rabbits
2) a bunny, cotton
3) the sky
4) a star, the sun

See page 288.

c. Try to think of words to complete the following similes:

1) The boys were jumping around like _____.
2) The blanket was soft like _____.
3) The water was blue like _____.
4) The light was bright like _____.

d. Write three to four similes on your own. If you need help, look back at your description in **4c**, and compare the flowers.

e. Optional: Take your spelling test today.

★

Review Activities

1. *Forming plurals*
   Write the plural, or the word which means more than one.

   a. baby
   b. jelly
   c. pansy
   d. copy

2. *Syllables*
   Divide the words into syllables.

   a. bubble
   b. trouble
   c. swimmer
   d. happen

3. *Similies*
   Complete these sentences with a simile.

   a. The kite rose high like _____.
   b. The flower was pretty like _____.

1.
a. babies
b. jellies
c. pansies
d. copies

2.
a. bub/ble
b. trou/ble
c. swim/mer
d. hap/pen

3. Possible answers
a. a cloud, a bird
b. a picture

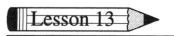
Teacher's Note:
As your student completes each lesson, choose skills from the *Review Activities* that he needs. The *Review Activities* follow each lesson.

Teacher's Note: If you choose to dictate, tell your student when to begin a new line. Also, tell him that in this poem, the first word in each line are capitalized.

I'll sail my boat tomorrow
In wonderful new places,
But first I'll take my watering pot
And wash the pansies' faces.

"Rain in the Night"
by Amelia Josephine Burr

1. a. Listen as your teacher reads the poem. Write this poem from dictation the second time she reads it, or copy it. Compare your copy to the poem and make corrections.

   b. Copy the spelling words from *Focus on Spelling*. Say the words aloud as you write them. Notice that these words spell the /ā/ sound with **ai**.

See page 288.

2.
a. Three syllables

> ### Focus on Spelling
> sail   wait   plain   raise   hair
> **Bonus Word:** tomorrow

2. a. We can count the number of syllables in a word by clapping for each syllable we hear. Say the word *tomorrow* for your teacher, and clap each sound you hear. How many syllables do you hear?

b. to/mor/row

   b. We heard three syllables in the word *tomorrow*. Now let's look at the word. Where would you divide the word *tomorrow*? Most syllables have a consonant and a vowel sound, or consonant-vowel-consonant together. Look at how you divided your word into syllables. Check to make sure you divided it by the sounds you heard.

c. won/der/ful, wa/ter/ing

   c. Do the same with the words *wonderful* and *watering*. Listen as your teacher says them, then say and clap the words. Divide the words into syllables on your paper by drawing lines between the syllables.

d. 1) yes/ter/day
    2) af/ter/noon
    3) be/gin/ning
    4) cov/er/ing

   d. Longer words are not necessarily harder. Divide these three syllable words.
   Ex: re/mem/ber

   1) yesterday   2) afternoon   3) beginning   4) covering

e. **SEE-SPELL-SAY:** Look and **see** each of the words on the spelling list. **Spell** each word aloud. **Say** the word.

3. a. The apostrophe is a mark that looks like this: (**'**).
An apostrophe is used in contractions to take the place of a missing letter(s). Circle each word in the poem with an apostrophe.

b. An **apostrophe** is also used to show that something belongs to something or someone.
Ex: I borrowed my brother's bike.
The bike belongs to my brother.
Brother's is a singular possessive noun.
A singular possessive noun is a singular noun with an apostrophe and **s** (**'s**) to show that it possesses something.

Punctuation Pointer	**Grammar Guide**
Apostrophe - Use an apostrophe **s** (**'s**) to show that something belongs to something or someone.	**Singular possessive noun** - a singular noun with an apostrophe **s** (**'s**) to show that something belongs to something or someone

Look at these phrases with your teacher. Circle the **'s** in each phrase.

1) the dog's dish   5) the cat's claws
2) Mother's coat   6) Bob's hat
3) the boy's bike   7) Dad's tie
4) Ann's doll   8) the dog's tail

c. Orally or in writing, answer each question using the phrases above:

1) What belongs to the dog?
2) What belongs to Mother?
3) What belongs to the boy?
4) What belongs to Ann?
5) What belongs to the cat?
6) What belongs to Bob?
7) What belongs to Dad?
8) What belongs to the dog?

3.
d. Answers will vary.

✎ **Teacher's Note:**
If the student's name ends with an s, just add an apostrophe.

e. faces

f. 1) ladies' hats
2) clocks' hands
3) sisters' toys
4) friends' houses

4.
b. wonderful, new
Possible answers:
sturdy, new, red, etc.

d. Make up three phrases telling about things that belong to you. Use your name, add **'s**, and then tell the name of something that belongs to you.
Ex: Bill's bike

e. You learned in Lesson 12 that the word *pansy* is singular (meaning one), and the word *pansies* is plural (meaning more than one). In this week's literature passage, the plural word *pansies'* has an apostrophe to tell us that something belongs to the pansies. This is a plural possessive noun, a plural noun with an apostrophe to show that it possesses something. What belongs to them?

> **Grammar Guide**
>
> **Plural possesive noun -**
> a plural noun with an apostrophe
> (') to show that something belongs
> to something or someone

f. We put an apostrophe after a plural word that ends with **s** to show that something belongs to that naming word, or noun. This is also called a plural possessive noun.

Write the correct way to show these things:
Ex: collars belonging to dogs - dogs' collars

1) hats belonging to ladies
2) hands belonging to clocks
3) toys belonging to sisters
4) houses belonging to friends

g. Practice your spelling words in a Spelling Bee.

4. a. Adjectives are describing words that help us understand more about people, places, and things. You learned about adjectives in Lesson 11. Review the work you did.

b. Look at the literature passage. Underline the two adjectives that describe the places where the boat will sail. Think of at least two adjectives to describe the boat.

c. Use the word card page in the *Student Activity Book* or write
    the following nouns and adjectives on index cards. Mix up
    each group of cards and place the nouns face down on one
    side and the adjectives face down on the other. Take turns
    turning over one noun and one adjective. If the two words go
    together, you get another turn.

Nouns		Adjectives	
car	boat	dark	new
rain	night	old	black
sky	dog	red	loud
baby	candy	hot	quiet
hat	fish	slow	big

d. Choose two of the noun/adjective pairs, and write a complete
    sentence with each pair. Remember to begin your sentence
    with a capital letter and end with a period.

e. Take your oral or written spelling pretest today.

★ ——————————————————————

5. a. We have now completed the lessons on the four verses of the
       poem entitled "Rain in the Night" by Amelia Josephine Burr.
       Begin to memorize the verse in this lesson by reading each
       line out loud. After you read each line out loud a few times,
       cover the first line and try to remember it. Repeat this
       process with each line.

   b. Present the poem, with the illustrations you have drawn, to a
       group. Remember to speak slowly and clearly so that you
       can be easily understood. Hold your illustrations in front of
       you as you speak. If you are uncomfortable speaking in front
       of others, you may want to practice in front of a mirror or
       speak into a tape or video recorder.

   c. Optional: Take your spelling test today.

★ ——————————————————————

c. Possible answers:
dark night, big dog,
quiet baby, slow car,
black fish, etc.

d. Example:
The new car belongs
to Joe.

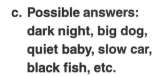

See page 288.

See page 288.

Review Activities

1. *Syllables*
   Divide these words into syllables.

   a. yesterday
   b. covering

2. *Singular Possessive nouns*
   Write the possessive form using an apostrophe.
   Ex: the dish belongs to the dog - <u>the dog's dish</u>

   a. the hat belongs to Mom
   b. the car belongs to Tom
   c. the bike belongs to the boy

3. *Plural possessive nouns*
   Write the plural possessive form using an apostrophe.
   Ex: the dishes belong to the dogs - <u>the dogs' dishes</u>

   a. the toys belong to the friends
   b. the cars belong to the brothers
   c. the flowers belong to the ladies

1.
a. yes/ter/day
b. cov/er/ing

2.
a. Mom's hat
b. Tom's car
c. boy's bike

3.
a. friends' toys
b. brothers' cars
c. ladies' flowers

Assessment 3
(Lessons 10 - 13)

1.
a. grew
b. ran
c. hop

1. Circle the verb, or doing word, in these sentences.
   a. That tree grew tall.
   b. The boy ran quickly.
   c. I hop on one foot.

2. Possible answers:
a. dull, dark
b. big, large
c. never, sometimes

2. Write an antonym, or a word of opposite meaning, for these words.
   a. bright
   b. little
   c. always

3.
a. loud
b. silly
c. happy

3. Circle the adjectives, or describing words.
   a. the loud noise
   b. the silly boy
   c. the happy mom

4.
a. mid/dle
b. trou/ble
c. fun/nel
d. to/mor/row
e. cir/cle
f. yes/ter/day

4. Divide these words into syllables.
   a. middle
   b. trouble
   c. funnel
   d. tomorrow
   e. circle
   f. yesterday

5.
a. babies
b. ladies
c. jellies

5. Write the plural, or the word that means more than one.
   a. baby
   b. lady
   c. jelly

6.
a. Joe's book
b. man's boat

6. Write the possessive noun.
   a. the book belongs to Joe
   b. the boat belongs to the man

7.
a. boys' cars
b. sisters' dog

7. Write the plural possessive noun.
   a. the cars belong to the boys
   b. the dogs belong to the sisters

Literature Link

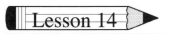

Madeline
by Ludwig Bemelman
Published by
Penguin Group

Literature Link

1. There are two options for this week's lesson.

   Option 1 - Get the book, *Madeline,* by Ludwig Bemelman, from the library and read half of the story today.

Summary
Madeline

This story is about twelve little girls who live in a big house with their mistress, Miss Clavel. Miss Clavel and her twelve girls do and see many things in the great city of Paris. The smallest of the twelve girls is Madeline. She is a brave, daring, little girl. One night, Miss Clavel finds Madeline in bed, crying. The doctor says that she must have an appendectomy, which means she must have her appendix removed. The little girls miss Madeline, and one day they go to visit her. They find that Madeline has a lovely room with lots of toys, but most importantly, she has a scar on her stomach. The little girls are very impressed with everything that Madeline has received. When Miss Clavel puts the eleven other little girls to bed that night, she discovers that now they are all crying. They have all decided that they want to have their appendixes out.

Option 2 - Listen to your teacher as she reads the French words to you. Read half of the story, "A Jeune Fille Named Marie."

French Vocabulary

jeune fille *(zhun fee)* - *girl*
famille *(fa-mee)* - *family*
frere *(rhymes with "where")* - *brother*
metro (me-tro) - *subway*
maison (may-zon) - *house*
Bois de Bologne (Bwa de Bu-lon-ya) - *Woods of Bologne*
velos (ve-lo rhymes with "hello") - *bicycle*
Tour de France (Tour rhymes with "poor") -a yearly race
la glace (la-glas) - *ice cream*
au chocolate (oh shock-o-lat) - *chocolate*
la glace a la fraise (a la frays) - *strawberry ice cream*
merci (mare-see) - *thank you*
au revoir (oh re-vwa) - *goodbye*
allo (ah-low) - *hello*

A Jeune Fille Named Marie

Marie lives in a city called Paris. Paris is the biggest city in France. Marie and her **famille** like to visit all the wonderful places in town. She goes with her mother, father, and **frere**. His name is Pierre. Marie and Pierre like to ride the bus and the **metro**.

Pierre plays **football** (*soccer*), and Marie loves to dance. They go from their **maison** to the park to play. Their favorite park is the **Bois de Bologne**. Many of the parks and gardens in Paris were built for the kings and queens of France only. Now all the people of Paris may enjoy these parks.

At the parks, Marie and Pierre also ride their **velos**. Many people in France like to ride their bikes. A race is held every year called the **Tour de France**. People all over the world watch this race on T.V. It takes a long time to finish. The winner is a big star in France.

After they play, Marie and Pierre like to have a snack. Mother brings them **la glace**. Pierre likes **la glace au chocolate** best. Marie likes **la glace a la fraise** best. Pierre and Marie tell mother **merci** for the snack. Then it is time to go home. It has been a fun and busy day.

As Marie, Pierre, Father, and Mother go back home, it is time to say **au revoir**. If you go to France, you can use some of the new words you have learned. If you ever meet someone from France, be sure to say **allo**!

2.

b. *Madeline*

1) She lives in Paris, France.

2) Miss Clavel and eleven other little girls

3) Her appendix had to be removed, so she had to be taken to the hospital.

4) Miss Clavel and the girls

5) The scar on her stomach

6) All the little girls wanted to get their appendixes out.

7) They thought it was fun to have presents and a scar.

8) She told them to thank the Lord that they were well and to go to sleep.

2.

b. "A Jeune Fille Named Marie"

1) The story is about Marie, Mother, Father, and her brother, Pierre.

2) They live in Paris, France.

3) They ride the bus, the metro, and bicycles.

4) Pierre likes football, and Marie likes to dance.

5) The first parks were built for the kings and queens of France.

6) They like to ride their *velos*, or bicycles. The famous bike race in France is called the Tour de France.

7) Pierre's favorite snack is chocolate ice cream. Marie's favorite snack is strawberry ice cream.

8) *Allo!* and *Au revoir!*

2. a. Continue the book or story from yesterday.

b. Discuss the following questions with your teacher.

Discussion Questions for *Madeline*:

1) Where does Madeline live?
2) Who does Madeline live with?
3) What problem did Madeline have?
4) Who came to visit Madeline?
5) What was the surprise that Madeline showed her friends?
6) What was Miss Clavel's next problem?
7) Why did the little girls want to have an operation?
8) What did Miss Clavel say to the little girls when they cried?

Discussion Questions for "A Jeune Fille Named Marie":

1) Who is this story about? Name the four people told about in the story.
2) What city do Pierre and Marie live in? What country do they live in? What city and country do you live in?
3) How do Pierre and Marie travel around in Paris? How do you travel around the place you live?
4) What is Pierre's favorite sport? What does Marie like to do? What do you like to do for fun?
5) Pierre and Marie went to a park with their parents. Who were the parks first built for?
6) What do Marie and Pierre like to ride? Do you like to ride your bike? What is the famous race for cyclists in France called?
7) Snacks are good after you play. What is Pierre's favorite snack? What is Marie's favorite snack? What is your favorite snack?
8) What would you say to someone you meet who speaks French? What would you say when he leaves?

c. Here is a map of Paris.

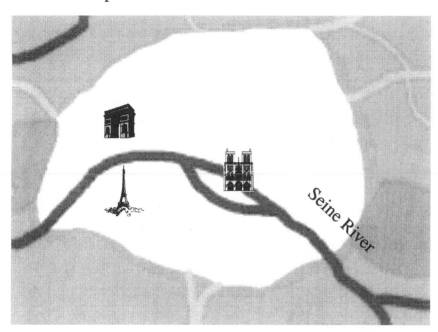

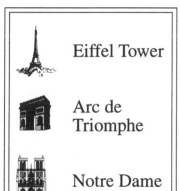

Eiffel Tower

Arc de Triomphe

Notre Dame

Locate the following places on your map:
1) Eiffel Tower
2) Cathedral of Notre Dame (No-tru Dam)
3) Arc de Triomphe (Ark de Tree-omffe)

d. These are all famous places in Paris. Look up these three sites in an encyclopedia (see France or Paris), or read the information given below. Write the names under the correct pictures.

 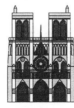

Eiffel Tower - Built for the World's Fair in 1889, this tower is now the symbol for Paris. It is 984 feet high.

The Cathedral of Notre Dame - This cathedral (church) was finished in the year 1263. It is located on an island in the center of Paris, called the Isle de la Cite (Eel-de-la-See-Tay). The stained glass windows of this cathedral are beautiful, with its rose windows being world famous. Victor Hugo's novel, *The Hunchback of Notre Dame*, was written about this place.

Arc de Triomphe - The Arch of Triumph, as it is known, is located at the Place de l'Etoile (the Place of the Star). Twelve avenues come together at the Place de l'Etoile (plas-de-le-twah), forming a star shape. The Arch of Triumph is the largest and most well-known stone arch in the world. It was begun by the Emperor Napoleon in 1806, as a monument to his victories. It was completed in 1836 and dedicated to "All French armies since 1792." The burial place of France's Unknown Soldier is there.

2. f.

🖉 **Teacher's Note:**
Page numbers may not be noted in your publication of *Madeline*. Therefore the page numbers indicated assume that the first page of the story is page 1. A description of the picture is noted.

2.
f. 1) Page 6; Miss Clavel and the girls are looking at a carriage horse.
2) Page 7; Miss Clavel and the girls frown at a thief.
3) Page 10; Miss Clavel and the girls are walking in the rain.
4) Page 14; Miss Clavel and the girls are ice skating.
5) Page 22; The ambulance is taking Madeline to the hospital.

e. After listening to your teacher read the information, or after reading it yourself, tell the importance of each site.

f. **Optional:** Locate the following places in Ludwig Bemelman's book, *Madeline*:
1) The Opera
2) Place Vendome
3) The Cathedral of Notre Dame
4) The Basilica of Sacre-Coeur
5) Eiffel Tower

3.
a. Allow for discussion.

3. a. Many children live in countries other than America. Talk with your teacher about things that may be the same (compare) and things that may be different (contrast) with children in other countries.

Discuss these things that are similar for all children.
1) Families
2) Need for food and clothing
3) School or learning
4) Play

b. Allow for discussion.

b. While all children have things in common, there are also many things that are different. Talk with your teacher about the ways life may be different for children in countries other than America:

1) Language
2) Customs
3) Religion
4) Need to work
5) Opportunities for the future

c. Find pictures from magazines or catalogs of children from different countries. Get a piece of construction or drawing paper, and glue these pictures on it. This is called a *collage*. Try to find as many different aged children as you can.

d. On the back of your collage, make two headings like this:

Same   **Different**

Now make a list of the ways you are the same as the children in your collage and ways that you are different. Include at least four items on each list.

e. **Optional:** You may want to pick a foreign country and find out what life is like for a child in that country. Ask your teacher for help in finding reference material.

4. a. Find each of the words in the box in the wordsearch. Circle the word in the box after you have found it in the wordsearch. Remember that words can go from top to bottom or from side to side.

Ex: The word *big* is inside this wordsearch going from top to bottom. *Dog* is in here going from left to right. Words can share letters. *Big* and *dog* share the letter **g**.

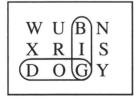

Look at the first few letters of your word to try to find it. Ask your teacher for help if you have trouble completing this activity.

Teacher's Note:
Children who are sponsored by missionary associations are usually from foreign countries. You may want to talk with someone who sponsors a missionary child or investigate having your family or church sponsor one.

b. Find these words in the word search from our story, "A Jeune Fille Named Marie." Remember, the words run top to bottom or left to right.

Word Search I

frere	Paris	famille
favorite	Marie	maison

4. b. Word Search I

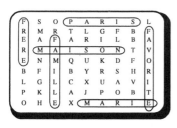

F	S	O	P	A	R	I	S	L
R	M	R	T	L	G	F	B	L
E	A	F	A	R	I	L	B	F
R	M	A	I	S	O	N	T	A
E	N	M	Q	U	K	D	F	V
B	F	I	B	Y	R	S	H	O
L	G	L	C	X	U	A	V	R
P	K	L	A	J	P	O	B	I
O	H	E	X	M	A	R	I	E

Word Search II

Pierre	France	metro
velo	glace	allo

Word Search II

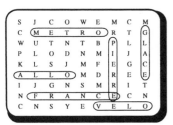

S	J	C	O	W	E	M	C	M
C	M	E	T	R	O	R	T	G
W	U	T	N	T	B	P	L	G
P	L	O	D	N	M	I	J	L
K	L	S	J	M	F	E	G	A
A	L	L	O	M	D	R	E	C
I	J	G	N	S	M	R	I	E
N	F	R	A	N	C	E	C	T
C	N	S	Y	E	V	E	L	N
C	N	S	Y	E	V	E	L	O

c. Tell your teacher what each of the French words mean.

1) frere   4) velo   7) allo
2) famille   5) metro
3) maison   6) la glace

d. You have been introduced to lists of spelling words in
    Lessons 7-13. Review these spelling words.

5. a. Either orally or in writing, spell the following words for your
        teacher:

1) follow   The dog will *follow* his owner.
2) wear   What will you *wear* to the party?
3) leave   We have to *leave* for the store.
4) third   I am in the *third* grade this year.
5) wait   Mother wants us to *wait* for her.
6) count   How high can you *count*?
7) somewhere   The toy is *somewhere* in your room.
8) night   The lights come on at *night*.

b. Listen to your teacher as she dictates a sentence to you.

    Always leave the ground clean.

c. After your teacher has checked your sentence, make any
    corrections.

    Cover your paper so that you can not see your corrected
    sentence. Listen again to your teacher as she dictates the
    same sentence again. Repeat the correction process.

---

c. 1) brother
    2) family
    3) house
    4) bicycle
    5) bus
    6) ice cream
    7) hello

✏ **Teacher's Note: You may read the sentences if your student needs them to understand the words given.**

✏ **Teachers Note: Read the sentence to your student to be written from dictation. Read slowly, repeating it several times. Encourage your student to just listen the first time, and then begin. Do not be concerned about saying it too often. The goal is for your student to be able to write the sentence. Speed and accuracy will be increased over time.**

✏ **Teacher's Note: After your student's first attempt, show him how to correct any mistakes. Read the sentence again several times if needed. Repeat the correction process. Make sure to praise improvements. He may attempt it a third time if he desires; however, be alert to fatigue. If your student is overly tired or discouraged at this point, it is best to end the session, highlighting improvements.**

I C.A.N. Assessment
for the
Literature Link on Paris

After the *Literature Link* is completed, check off each I C.A.N. objective with your teacher.

C
    I can **complete** my work.
    I can be **creative**.

A
    I can be **accurate**.
    I can do my work with a good **attitude**.

N
    I can do my work **neatly**.

EVERYDAY WORDS

New Skills

Reporting	Graphs
Pronoun	Map Skills
Charts	Newspaper
Compass	Tally Marks
Directions	Facts

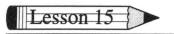

Teacher's Note:
As your student completes each lesson, choose skills from the *Review Activities* that he needs. The *Review Activities* follow each lesson.

Teacher's Note:
Have a newspaper available for your student to use during this lesson.

Teacher's Note:
For lesson 16 you will need a map of your town a state to complete the activities.

See page 288.

 *A record 5.7 million people visited the Eiffel Tower, France's most popular tourist attraction, in 1990.*

From *The Tampa Tribune*, Feb. 3, 1991

1. a. Listen as your teacher reads the literature passage. Looking at the passage, read the sentence along with your teacher. Copy the passage. Compare your copy to the literature passage and make corrections.

    b. Copy the spelling words from *Focus on Spelling*. Say the words aloud as you write them. Notice that the /**w**/ or /**h**/ sound at the beginning of each word is spelled **wh**.

> ### Focus on Spelling
> who   what   when   where   why
> **Bonus Word:** reporter

2. a. Look at your newspaper. With your teacher's help, find the name of your newspaper. This is called the banner. Look at the front page and find the main, or largest, headline. With your teacher's help, read the headline. Tell your teacher what you think the main story will be about.

> **Using Your Tools**
>
> The **newspaper** gives you current events, weather, sports, and much more.

    b. Look at the newspaper with your teacher. With her help, look at the index to find the following sections:
      1) Sports   3) Editorials   5) Classified Section
      2) World   4) Comics

    Talk with your teacher about the type of information you see in each section.

c. After looking at a newspaper, tell your teacher your favorite section. What do you think your mother's favorite part would be? Your father's? Look at the index, and try to find the weather report. Show it to your teacher, and tell her what you think the weather will be like tomorrow.

d. Choose two or three pictures you like from the newspaper. With your teacher, read the caption, or words telling about the picture. Try to think of your own description for each picture. Write it yourself, or tell it to your teacher so she can write it down.

e. **SEE-SPELL-SAY:** Look and **see** each word from the spelling list. **Spell** each word aloud. **Say** the word.

3. a. In Lesson 13, you learned about using an apostrophe to show that something belongs to a noun. In your literature passage, there is a word that uses an apostrophe to show that something belongs to it. Underline that word.

b. In your literature passage, the word *France's* shows that something belongs to France. What belongs to France?

c. Look at the three sets of sentences. Some of the italicized words need apostrophes, and some are just plural nouns. Look at each set and decide which of the italicized words need an apostrophe added.
Copy that sentence, and add the apostrophe.

1) The *dogs* love to play with the ball.
Bring the *dogs* water dish into the house.

2) It is good to read a lot of *books*.
Look at that *books* cover.

3) I went with my mother to pick out my *fathers* new shirt.
Both of my roomates sent their *fathers* a present.

d. Practice your spelling words in a Spelling Bee.

★ ———————————

3.
a. France's

b. Most popular tourist attraction (the Eiffel Tower)

✐ **Teacher's Note:**
All words which need an apostrophe are singular possessive nouns.
Ex: "dog's water dish,"
not "dogs' water dish."

c. 1) Bring the *dog's* water dish into the house.
2) Look at that *book's* cover.
3) I went with my mother to pick out my *father's* new shirt.

——— **See page 289.**

4.

a. attraction

b. 1) va/ca/<u>tion</u>
   2) col/lec/<u>tion</u>
   3) pol/lu/<u>tion</u>
   4) sta/<u>tion</u>
   5) at/trac/<u>tion</u>
   6) cap/<u>tion</u>

d. 1) pollution
   2) vacation
   3) collection
   4) station
   5) caption
   6) attraction

See page 289.

5.

a. 5.7 million people visited the Eiffel Tower in 1990.

The Eiffel Tower is in Paris, France.

It was France's most popular tourist attraction.

---

4. a. When we see the letters **-tion**, they often say /**shun**/. Circle the word in our passage with the letters **-tion**.

Phonics Fact
-tion says /**shun**/

  b. Listen as your teacher reads this list of words. Then, underline the letters in each word that say /**shun**/. Also, after hearing the list of words read, draw lines dividing the words into syllables.

    1) vacation   3) pollution   5) attraction
    2) collection   4) station   6) caption

  c. Look at the words divided into syllables. What do you notice about the letters **-tion**? The letters **-tion** make up one syllable. Orally make up sentences using each of the **-tion** words in **4b**. Tell your teacher what you think each word means. Using your dictionary, look up any words you don't know.

  d. Use your **-tion** words from **4b** to fill in the blanks in these sentences, either orally or in writing:

    1) The river is not clean because of _____.
    2) We are going on a family _____to the beach.
    3) Bob will add another baseball card to his _____.
    4) We must go to the gas _____to get gas for the car.
    5) There is a _____under the picture telling what it is.
    6) The best _____is the big ride at the fair.

  e. Take your oral or written spelling pretest today.

5. a. Our passage is taken from a newspaper article. News articles are written differently than other stories because they have to tell many things in a small space. What facts, or true statements, do you see in our literature passage? Make a written list of the facts.

b. With your teacher, choose a newspaper article to read. After reading, find three facts, or true statements, that are in your news article. Use a highlighter pen to mark them.

c. After reading the article or story, you can remember most of the basic information if you ask yourself the following questions:

1) **Who** is the article about?
2) **What** happened in the article?
3) **When** did the story take place?
4) **Where** did the story take place?
5) **Why** was the story written? What did the person who wrote the story want people to know?

These questions are called the 5-W questions:
Who? **What**? **When**? **Where**? **Why**?
Use these questions when you are writing to help you gather important information.

d. Think of an event you know about such as a special family event, birthday party, or holiday celebration. Pretend you are a newspaper reporter and orally, or in writing, answer the following 5-W Questions. This would be the basis for an article about the event.

1) **Who** attended the event?
2) **What** event was being celebrated?
3) **When** did the event take place?
4) **Where** did the event take place?
5) **Why** was the event held?

Optional: If you want to write a story about this event, you may include pictures and captions as well.

e. Optional: Take your spelling test today.

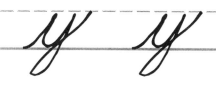

y y

z z

b   k

p   j

w   x

Review Activities

1. *Apostrophes*
   Read the sentences and decide which word needs an apostrophe. Write the apostrophe.

   a. The *cats* love that ball.
      This is the *cats* ball.

   b. The *books* cover is torn.
      Tom has six *books*.

2. *Listing facts*
   Read these sentences. List two facts.

   Science is the best subject. Today, I learned that the sun is very big. It gives us heat and light. I am glad we have the sun.

✐ **Teacher's Note:**
Explain to your student that *cats* in sentence *b* refers to one cat; *book* in sentence *c* refers to one book, if needed.

1.
a. This is the *cat's* ball.
b. The *book's* cover is torn.

2. The sun is very big.
   The sun gives us heat and light.

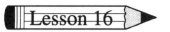

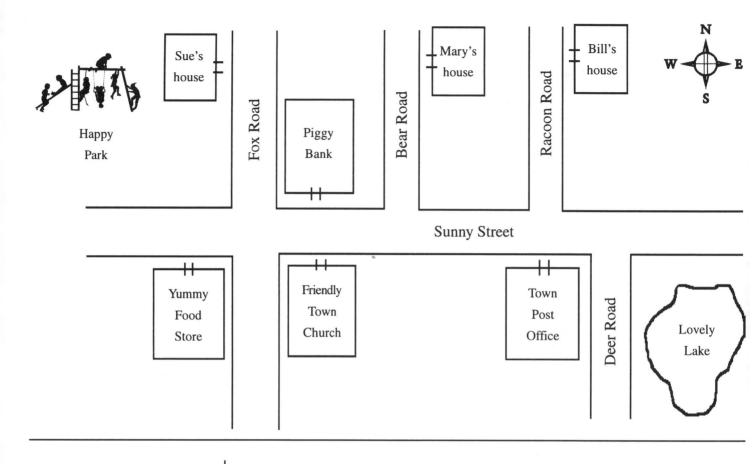

Teacher's Note:
A map of your town or state will be needed to complete this activity.

1. a. Here is a simple map of Friendly Town. On our map you can find streets, buildings, lakes, and parks.

Using Your Tools

A **map** is a picture that shows the location of things and places.

Looking at your map, locate the following places:

1) Friendly Town businesses
2) Places to play
3) People's houses
4) Names of the streets

b. Now go back, and using colored pencils, color each of the locations with the following colors:
1) Friendly Town businesses - red
2) Places to play - green
3) People's houses - blue
4) Names of the streets - gray

c. Using your map, make a list of at least two places for each category.
1) Friendly Town businesses
2) Places to play
3) People's houses
4) Names of the streets

2. a. On the map are some crossed lines with some capital letters. This is called a **compass**. What do you think the four letters stand for?

b. The four directions (north, south, east, and west) help us read maps and know which way to go. The arrows on the compass show us direction. For example, here are directions from Yummy Food Store to Bill's house: "Go east down Sunny Street and then turn north on Raccoon Road."

Tell your teacher the directions for these trips:
1) Friendly Town Church to Mary's house
2) Bill's house to Happy Park
3) Lovely Lake to Sue's house
4) Piggy Bank to Town Post Office

c. With your teacher, figure out which direction your house faces (north, south, east, or west). The best way to remember directions is by remembering that the sun rises in the east and sets in the west. When you face east, north will be on your left, and south will be on your right. Determine the direction (north, south, east, or west) of two or three places from your house.

★ ——————————————————

3. a. Look at the map of your town or state. With your teacher, find things such as the town or street where you live, court house or state capital, symbols for roads, rivers, parks, etc., and the compass on the map.

---

c. 1) **Yummy Food Store, Piggy Bank, Town Post Office**
2) **Lovely Lake, Happy Park**
3) **Sue's house, Mary's house, Bill's house**
4) **Sunny Street, Fox Road, Bear Road, Raccoon Road, Deer Road**

2.
a. **N - north, S - south, E - east, W - west**

b. 1) **East on Sunny Street, north on Bear Road**
2) **South on Raccoon Road, west on Sunny Street**
3) **North on Deer Road, west on Sunny Street, north on Fox Road**
4) **East on Sunny Street**

See page 289.

b. Find at least one example for each of the following features on your state or town map.

1) river   4) airport
2) park   5) road
3) mountain (or other landform)

c. Discuss symbols or features on the map that are interesting to you. Choose something you do not recognize, and find out what it means.

See page 289.

4.

a. They start with capital letters.

4. a. Proper nouns are specific people, places, or things. Proper nouns begin with a capital letter. Here are some examples: New York, Mrs. Jones, Friday. Show your teacher examples of specific places on your map. How do the names of these places start?

b. There are names of three specific people on the map of Friendly Town. Find their names on your map and underline them.

b. Sue, Mary, Bill.

c. Write your entire name. What kind of letter does your name start with? What about your middle name?

c. First, middle, and last names start with capital letters.

d. Specific names of people, places, and things start with capital letters. They are called proper nouns. Capitalize days of the week, months, holidays, and specific products as well as specific names of people, places, and things.

> ### Grammar Guide
>
> A **proper noun** names a particular person, place, or thing.
> Begin a proper noun with a **capital letter**.

d. Possible Answers
  1) Monday, Sunday
  2) May, April
  3) Easter, Thanksgiving
  4) Ford, Kleenex

Write two names for each category. Make sure they start with capital letters.

1) Days of the week
2) Months
3) Holidays
4) Specific products you can buy

See page 289.

5. a. Choose a location on our Friendly Town map and draw
   your house. Try to make your house about the same size as
   the other houses. Think about where you would like to live
   before you choose your location. Write your name,
   apostrophe and **s** ('**s**) and the word *house* on the house.

   Ex: Ron's house

   b. Anyone can draw a map. With your teacher's help, draw a
   map of your room or house. Decide the shape of the room or
   house and then draw in things like doors and windows.
   You may also add things like furniture, rugs, and lamps.
   It can be as simple or as detailed as you want it to be. It may
   take several tries to make it look like you want, so don't get
   discouraged.

   Ex:

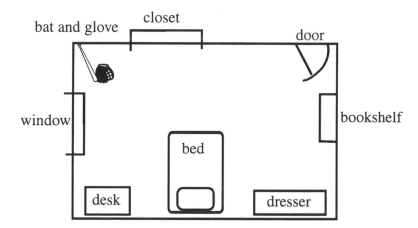

Review Activities

1.
a. **Notre Dame**
b. **Arc de Triomphe**

2.

3.
   Possible answers:
a. **January, February, etc.**
b. **Ron, Tracy, etc.**
c. **Paris, New York, etc.**

1. *Directions*
   Use the map of Paris in Lesson 14 to answer these questions.

   a. What is east of the Eiffel Tower?
   b. What is north of the Eiffel Tower?

2. *Directions*
   Fill in the compass with north, south, east, and west.

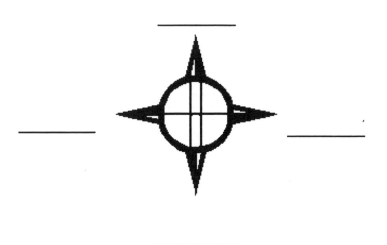

3. *Proper Nouns*
   Write two proper nouns for each word.

   a. months
   b. boy's names
   c. cities

Jesus kept growing taller and wiser.
He loved others, and many people
loved Him. Jesus always did what
pleased God, His heavenly Father.

Bible Stories to Read by Martha Rohrer.
Used by permission, Rod and Staff, Inc.
Crockett, Kentucky 41413

Bible Stories to Read by Martha Rohrer.
Used by permission, Rod and Staff, Inc.
Crockett, Kentucky 41413

1. a. Listen as your teacher reads the literature passage. Write the literature passage from dictation the second time she reads them, or copy it. Compare your copy to the literature passage and make corrections.

   b. Copy the spelling words from *Focus on Spelling*. Say the words aloud as you write them. Some words spell the /e/ sound with **ea**. Some words spell the /o/ sound at the end of a word with **ow**.

Focus on Spelling

please   pleased   pleasing   grow   growing
Bonus Word: *heavenly*

★ ————————————————————

2. a. You can add a suffix or extra letter(s) to the end of a word to show that the word's meaning has changed. When you add the suffix **-er** to the end of an adjective, or describing word, you show that the meaning of the word is happening to a greater degree.

   After my bath, I will be cleaner.

   The suffix **-er** shows a greater degree of being clean than before. Underline the words in the literature passage that have the suffix **-er**.

   b. Look at the two **-er** words from our literature passage.

                 taller   wiser

   Tell your teacher a rule for adding **-er** to a word ending in a silent **e**.

Teacher's Note:
As your student completes each lesson, choose skills from the *Review Activities* that he needs. The *Review Activities* follow each lesson.

Teacher's Note:
Tell your student that we capitalize *Him, His,* and *Father* because they are words referring to God. This will be covered in a higher level book.

See page 289.

2.
a. taller, wiser

b.
If the word ends in a silent *e*, drop the *e* and add *-er*.

2.

c. 1) slower
  2) riper
  3) faster
  4) nicer
  5) grayer
  6) whiter

d. 1) slower
  2) grayer
  3) riper
  4) nicer
  5) whiter
  6) faster

3.

a. Jesus loved others,
  and many people
  loved Jesus.

b. 1) We
  2) you
  3) She
  4) it
  5) They
  6) me

> ### Grammar Guide
>
> To add **-er** to most words, just add **-er**.
> To add **-er** to a word ending with a
> silent **e**, drop the **e** and add **-er**.

c. Rewrite these words, adding the suffix **-er** to each word:

  1) slow   3) fast   5) gray
  2) ripe   4) nice   6) white

d. Fill in these sentences with the words you made in **2c**.

  1) The tortoise is _____ than the hare, but he won the race.
  2) The gray clouds became _____ as the storm approached.
  3) Mary's banana is _____ than mine.
  4) The weather is _____ today than yesterday.
  5) The clean sheets look _____ than snow.
  6) I can run _____ than Mom.

e. **SEE-SPELL-SAY:** Look and **see** each of the spelling words on the spelling list. **Spell** each word aloud. **Say** the word.

3. a. Read the first two sentences in the literature passage. In the second sentence, two words are used that mean Jesus. These words, *He* and *Him*, are called pronouns. Pronouns are used so we don't say the person's name over and over. Read the second sentence again, replacing Jesus for *He* and *Him*. Which sounds better to you?

> ### Grammar Guide
>
> **Pronoun** - a word which
> takes place of a noun

b. Pronouns are used in place of nouns. Find the pronoun in each sentence and underline it.

  1) We will go to the park.
  2) Are you and Mother going to the store?
  3) She is wearing a blue dress.
  4) Bring it into the house.

5) They are waiting for the next bus.

6) Please give the book to me.

c. The pronoun *his* is a little different. It can show that something belonged to *someone*. Look at the last sentence in your literature passage. Why do you think the word *His* was used?

d. Practice your spelling words in your Spelling Bee today.

c. The word *His* takes the place of the word *Jesus*.

See page 289.

★ ————————————————————————

4. a. We can tell people we love them. Mothers and fathers and children say, "I love you" to each other often. Another way to say "I love you" without saying anything is to show someone you love him. How do you think you could show someone you love him?

4.

a. You could show someone you love them by doing things that please them.

b. Our literature passage describes Jesus as a child. Most children want to please their parents. Jesus wanted to please His earthly parents. Talking with your teacher, make a list of at least five things you can do that pleases your parents.

b. Answers will vary.

c. Jesus loved God His Father, so He wanted to please Him. Discuss with your teacher ways that you can show God you love Him. Make a list of at least five things you can do to please your heavenly Father.

c. Answers will vary.

d. Take your oral or written spelling pretest today.

See page 289.

★ ————————————————————————

5. a. Being able to read different kinds of charts and graphs is important. Here are three different kinds of charts and graphs with questions following each one.

First is a bar graph. It shows the number of oranges picked from the Smith family orange tree each year for four years. The height of each bar tells how many oranges were picked each year.

Oranges Picked from the Smith's Tree

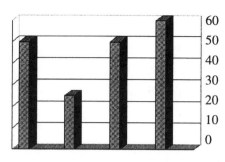

1993 1994 1995 1996

5.
a. 1) 1996
   60
   2) 1994
   25
   It is the number
   halfway between
   20 and 30.
   3) 1993 and 1995
   50 each year
   4) Possible Answers:
   - plant disease
   - weather
   - not enough people to
   pick the oranges

1) In what year were the most oranges picked?
   How many oranges were picked that year?

2) In what year were the lowest number of oranges picked?
   How many oranges were picked?

3) During two years, the same number of oranges were
   picked. What years were they? How many oranges were
   picked during those years?

4) Sometimes numbers don't tell the whole story. What
   reasons can you think of for why the Smith family only
   picked 25 oranges in 1994? Come up with at least three
   possible answers.

b. Here is another kind of chart. It shows us how many times
   each member of the Smith family swam during their vacation.
   This chart uses tally marks. Tally marks are made in groups
   of five.

   Here are four tally marks: | | | |
   Here are five tally marks: ╫╫

   The fifth tally mark is made across the first four. That way,
   when you count the marks, you can count by groups of five.

Swimming Trips on the Smith's Vacation
Dad   ⊤⊤⊤⊤ ||||
Mom   ⊤⊤⊤⊤ |||
Sam   ⊤⊤⊤⊤ ⊤⊤⊤⊤ ⊤⊤⊤⊤
Jill   ⊤⊤⊤⊤ ⊤⊤⊤⊤ ||||
Mike   ⊤⊤⊤⊤ ⊤⊤⊤⊤ |||

1) Who went swimming the most times during the Smith family vacation? How many times did this person swim?

2) Who went swimming the least number of times during the Smith family vacation? How many times did this person swim?

3) How many times did the boys (Dad included) swim? How many times did Jill and Mom swim altogether?

4) Think about the fun things you can do at a lake or the ocean. List at least three activities that the Smith family may have done on their vacation by the water. Tell why you think Sam Smith may have gone swimming so many times.

c. This next type of graph uses pictures to show the numbers it is reporting. The Smith children have a little business. They make and sell yo-yos. This graph shows the design and number of yo-yos they made.

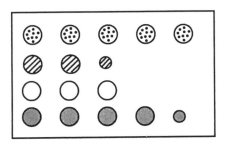

Key	⊛ = dotted
◯ = 10 yo-yos	⊘ = striped
○ = 5 yo-yos	◯ = plain
	⬤ = gray

1) What kind of yo-yo did the Smiths make the most? How many of this type did they make?

2) What kind of yo-yo did the Smiths make the least? How many of this type of yo-yo did they make?

5.
b. 1) Sam
   15
   2) Mom
   8
   3) 37
   22
   4) Possible Answers: swim, ski, snorkel, build sand castles, fish

5.
c. 1) dotted
   50
   2) striped
   25

113

5.

c.

  3) 55
    150

  4) Possible answers:
    They are cheaper;
    They were better;
    They were prettier, etc.

    Answers will vary.

3) How many striped and plain yo-yos did they make altogether? How many yo-yos did they make altogether?

4) What may be a reason the dotted yo-yo sold best? Do you think this would be a fun business for three children to have? Tell your teacher what kind of business you might like to have.

d. Make your own graph or chart. With your teacher's help, choose something you can tell about using this method. Here are some suggestions:

1) The main kinds of toys you have, and how many of each kind
   Ex: cars, trucks, boats, etc.
2) The number of books you have and the type of stories, or the size of the books
3) The number of houses on your street divided by their colors
4) The number of cars on your street divided by their colors

e. Optional: Take your spelling test today.

Handwriting: Connecting Letters
Some letters connect together very easily. If a letter has a tail that swoops up from the bottom line, then it is easy to connect it to some letters. Practice these connections.

am

at

an

as

al

em

et

en

es

el

im

it

in

is

il

Review Activities

1.
a. nicer
b. taller
c. riper
d. wiser

2.
a. He
b. I
c. They

3.
a. Emily
b. 16
c. Michael
d. 7
e. 27
f. 15

1. *Suffix -er*
   Add the suffix **-er**.

   a. nice
   b. tall
   c. ripe
   d. wise

2. *Pronouns*
   Circle the pronouns.

   a. He is early for dinner.
   b. Mom and I fixed chicken.
   c. They will bring rolls.

3. *Reading Graphs*
   Read the graph and answer the questions.

Cupcakes Decorated	
Anne	卌 卌 /
Emily	卌 卌 卌 /
Michael	卌 //
Quen	卌 ///

   a. Who decorated the most cupcakes?
   b. How many did he or she decorate?
   c. Who decorated the least cupcakes?
   d. How many did he or she decorate?
   e. How many cupcakes did Anne and Emily decorate altogether?
   f. How many cupcakes did Quen and Michael decorate altogether?

Assessment 4
(Lessons 15 - 17)

1. Read these sentences and decide which sentence needs an apostrophe. Write the apostrophe.

   a. The *dogs* like the food.
   b. Bring in the *dogs* food.

   c. The hats are for the *boys*.
   d. These are the *boys* hats.

2. List two facts about yourself.

3. Write two proper nouns for each word.

   a. holidays
   b. days of the week
   c. states

4. Add the suffix **-er** to these words.

   a. hard
   b. white
   c. nice
   d. soft

5. Circle the pronouns.

   a. They are happy.
   b. We like cake.
   c. She is nice.
   d. I am in a hurry.

✏ Teacher's Note:
Explain to your student that *dogs* in sentence *b* refers to one dog; *boys* in sentence *d* refers to more than one boy, if needed.

1.
a. Bring in the dog's food.
b. These are the boys' hats.

2. Answers will vary.

3. Possible answers
a. Christmas,
   New Year's Day, etc.
b. Monday, Tuesday, etc.
c. Alabama, Florida, etc.

4.
a. harder
b. whiter
c. nicer
d. softer

5.
a. They
b. We
c. She
d. I

Literature Link

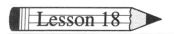

Literature Link

1. There are two options for this week's lesson:

Meet George Washington
by Joan Heilbroner
Published by Random
House

Option 1 - Find the book, *Meet George Washington,* by Joan Heilbroner, from the library and read half of the story today.

Summary
Meet George Washington

This book is called a biography because it tells about the life of a real person named George Washington. Taking the reader through George's years as a boy, you learn much about his love of riding and hunting, his schooling, and even his love for dance. Though he had many happy times, there were also hard times for George. By the time he became a soldier in his early twenties, George already knew about many things.

His early life prepared George for a lifetime of service to his country, first as a soldier, then as a statesman. After reading about his life, you can see how important he was to our country. This book takes you through his whole life and helps you get to know the "Father of Our Country."

Option 2 - Listen to your teacher as she reads the vocabulary words to you. Read the story, "George Washington's Journey."

Vocabulary			
soldier	important	special	president
Continental	American	honest	plantation
surveyor	Revolution	government	wealthy

George Washington's Journey

George Washington was a man who was very important to America. He was special for many reasons. He was the first president of our country. He led our army during the American Revolution. We think of him as the "Father of Our Country." Why was George Washington so special? It was the way he did great things. He was very brave and honest. He made other people feel important, too.

George was born on February 22, 1732 in Virginia. His father was a wealthy owner of a big plantation. George loved to play outside as a boy, and he liked to play sports. His favorite thing to do was riding horses. He became a very good rider. Life was good for George until his father died when he was eleven.

George moved to a place called Mount Vernon to live with his older brother, Lawrence. As he grew, he learned to do many things. When he was fourteen, he learned how to be a surveyor and went to the unsettled parts of our country. He saw Indians and many new things.

He was happy again until his brother Lawrence died when George was twenty. At this time, George joined the army. He became a very good soldier. He was helpful to his army. He fought with the English Army in the French and Indian War. In 1759, George married Martha Custis. She was a young widow with two children. George and Martha lived at Mount Vernon. George was happy taking care of his family and home.

In 1775, George again became a soldier. He was asked to be the leader of the Continental Army. This was the army of the thirteen colonies. This army had to fight the strong English Army. They were mostly just farmers and men from the woods. The people wanted to be free from the English king. The army led by General Washington had many hard times. They didn't have enough food or warm clothes, but George kept them together. After six years of fighting, the Continental Army won. In 1781, the American Revolution was over and the colonies were free.

George thought his work was over, so he went home to Mount Vernon. The young government of America was having trouble, so George went to Philadelphia to help. He helped write the Constitution. In 1789, he was elected the first president. He was president for eight years. He helped people learn how to work together and helped the government get started. George Washington was a good president.

In 1797, George went back home to Mount Vernon. He had served his country well. He had been a good soldier and leader. George Washington died on December 14, 1799. Many people loved and honored him. They thought he was a brave and honest leader. The people wanted to honor all that he did for America. They named the capital city after him, Washington, D.C.

2. a. Continue the book or story from yesterday.

   b. Discuss the following questions with your teacher.

Discussion Questions for "George Washington's Journey" or *Meet George Washington:*

1) When and where was George Washington born?
2) What was life like while George Washington's father was alive? What were George's favorite things to do as a boy?
3) When George was only fourteen, he began to work. What job did he do? How did life change again for George when he was twenty?
4) When George became a soldier, what army did he fight with? What was the first war he fought in?
5) What was George Washington's wife's name? Where did he and his family go to live?
6) In 1775, Washington became the head of a new army. What country did he fight for then? What kind of army did General Washington have to fight with?
7) General Washington showed his bravery and leadership many times. Finally, the American Revolution ended. What year did it end?
8) What was his last and very important job for his country? When did George Washington become our first president? How long did he remain president? What is the special name given to George Washington?

2.
a. 1) 1732, Virginia
2) George's life was good; his father was wealthy. George loved to play outdoors, play sports, and ride horses.
3) He was a surveyor. His brother, Lawrence, died, and he became a soldier.
4) He fought with the English army. The French and Indian War
5) Martha Custis Washington. He and his family went to Mount Vernon to live.
6) He fought for the Thirteen Colonies of America, the Colonial Army or the Continental Army. They were mostly untrained men such as farmers.
7) 1781
8) George Washington was the first president of the United States. He became the first president in 1789. He was president for eight years. The "Father of Our Country"

c. Match the events with the dates. Look back in your story if
you need help doing this activity.

Event	Dates
1) George Washington is born.	1743
2) George's father dies.	1752
3) George takes command of the Continental Army.	1775
4) George Washington dies.	1799
5) George's brother, Lawrence, dies.	1789
6) George is elected president.	1732
7) George marries Martha Custis.	1759

d. Answer the following questions about George's life:

1) How old was George Washington when he died?
2) How old was he when he was married?
3) How old was he when he became the leader of the
Continental Army?
4) How old was George Washington when he became the
first president?

3. a. Below is a list of activities done by George Washington.
Use the letters below to indicate when in his life these
activities may have been done.

B - Boyhood Years (0-12 years old)
Y - Young Man (13-21 years old)
M - Mature (Grown-Up) Man (22-50 years old)
O - Older Years (over 50 years old)

1) ___ George became a surveyor.
2) ___ George liked to play outside and ride horses.
3) ___ George married Martha Custis.
4) ___ George became our first president.
5) ___ George's father died.
6) ___ George became a soldier in the English Army.
7) ___ George was made leader of the Continental Army.
8) ___ George's army defeated the English to end the
American Revolution.
9) ___ George returned to Mount Vernon after being president.
10) ___ George's brother, Lawrence, died.

2.
c. 1) 1732
   2) 1743
   3) 1775
   4) 1799
   5) 1752
   6) 1789
   7) 1759

d. 1) 67 years old
   2) 27 years old
   3) 43 years old
   4) 56 years old

3.
a. 1) Y
   2) B
   3) M
   4) O
   5) B
   6) Y
   7) M
   8) M
   9) O
   10) Y

3.

b. 1) a person who is admired for things he has done and for his good qualities

2) a person who leads or directs others

3) not afraid, fearless

4) without lies, true to one's word

5) training of the character or mind

6) honor

c. Allow for discussion.

d. 1) honest
2) brave
3) leader
4) discipline
5) hero
6) dignity

4.
a. 1) Answers will vary.
2) It is important that George told the truth.
3) He was proud of him for telling the truth.

---

b. Look up these words in the dictionary. Discuss the meanings with your teacher and write a brief definition for each of them.

1) hero   4) honest
2) leader   5) discipline
3) brave   6) dignity

c. Tell how you think each of these words could apply to George Washington. Do you think these are good words to describe him?

d. Use these words from **3b** to fill in these blanks.

1) When George Washington would not tell a lie, he showed that he was _____.
2) When a soldier goes into battle, even if he is afraid, he must be _____.
3) When they needed a general for the army, they knew George would be a good _____.
4) George's _____ showed when he would work hard, not use bad language, and tell the truth.
5) After the Revolutionary War was over, everyone thought George was a _____.
6) The way George was fair with people and quietly led people by his actions showed great _____.

4. a. There is a story that was written about George Washington after his death. It told about an experience George may have had as a boy. As the story goes, George cut down his father's cherry tree with his hatchet. When his father asked him about it, George said, "I can not tell a lie. I chopped down the cherry tree." The story then tells of George's father hugging him. Since we don't know whether it is true or not, we can call it a legend about George Washington.

Answer these questions about this story:

1) Have you ever heard this story about George Washington?
2) What do you think is important about what George did in this story?

3) Why do you think his father hugged him?

4) Do you think George did the right thing? What would you have done?

5) This story points out a quality that George Washington had that made him a very good leader. What was that quality?

b. Draw a picture or pictures to show what happened in this story about George as a young boy. Make sure to include his hatchet (a small ax) and the cherry tree. These two things are symbols of this story.

c. Copy this Scripture on the back of your picture. Read it to your teacher, and discuss its meaning:

Do not let kindness and truth leave you;
Bind them around your neck,
Write them on the tablet of your heart.
So you will find favor and good repute
In the sight of God and man.

     Proverbs 3:3-4 (NASB)

5. You are going to give a presentation on George Washington. Use your activities and any pictures you drew or found to help you tell the story of his life. You may also want to use pictures from other books or encyclopedias.

To prepare for your presentation, you may answer the following questions as a guideline.

1) Who was George Washington?

2) What important things happened in his life?

3) Why is it important to know about George Washington?

4) What is your favorite part of George Washington's life?

5) What did you learn from George Washington?

Here are some more letters which connect together easily. The letters do not change. That is why they are easy to connect. Practice these connections:

4.

a. 4) Yes, George did the right thing.

5) Honesty

uh

up

uk

uf

uj

ah

ap

ak

af

aj

ha

pa

I C.A.N. Assessment
for the
Literature Link on George Washington

After the *Literature Link* is completed, check off each I C.A.N. objective with your teacher.

C   I can **complete** my work.
      I can be **creative**.

A   I can be **accurate**.
      I can do my work with a good **attitude**.

N   I can do my work **neatly**.

This page may be photocopied for student's use.

EVERYDAY WORDS

New Skills

Capitalization	Past Tense
Colon	Predicate
Comma	Quotations
Complete Sentence	Subject
Irregular Verb	Plays
Parentheses	Fact and Opinion

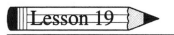
Teacher's Note:
Locate other children's plays at the library and read them to or with the student. Attending a play would be a wonderful illustration of our lesson.

An excerpt from the playlet:
"Jesus in the Temple"

Mary:　*Did you look in the temple?*

Joseph:　*No, I never thought to look there. It's just across the street. Let's go over there. (They cross the stage and seem to be looking in an open door.)*

Mary:　*Joseph, there he is sitting among all those teachers. Look how he is listening to them.*

> *Jesus, My Friend* by Helen Kitchell Evans.
> Used by permission of Shining Star Publications, a Division of Good Apple, Inc.
> Box 299, Carthage, Illinois, 62321-0299
> *This playlet is taken from the Scripture Luke 2:41-52.

1. a. These sentences are part of a **play**, or story, that is written so that people can act it out. Listen as your teacher reads the sentences, called **lines**. Read the lines with your teacher. Copy these sentences from the model.

   b. Copy the spelling words from *Focus on Spelling*. Say the words aloud as you write them. Some words spell the /ŏ/ sound with **ough**.

   ### Focus on Spelling
   thought　bought　brought　fought　ought
   Bonus Word: teacher

See page 289. ────────────────── ★

2.
a. Mary, Joseph

2. a. Let's look at the way the lines of a play are written. The names of the characters speaking are on the left followed by a colon (**:**). Underline in red the names of the people in the play. Who are the characters in this play?

Punctuation Pointer

Colon - a colon (**:**) is used in a play after a character's name, before his lines

---

b. What do we find after the colon (**:**)? Written among the words to be spoken by the characters are stage directions. These are surrounded by **parentheses** ( ). Find the stage directions and underline them in blue.

c. Learning when to speak in a play can sometimes be confusing. Using two different colored pencils (yellow and green), underline the words spoken by the characters. Underline in yellow the words spoken by Mary and the words spoken by Joseph in green.

d. Find a partner and choose parts (either Mary or Joseph) and read the play. Remember to only read your part and not to read stage directions aloud. After reading, trade parts. Try to read your part as though you were that person. This can be done as a play, puppet show, or flannel board story.

e. **SEE-SPELL-SAY:** Look and **see** each word in the spelling list. **Spell** each word aloud. **Say** the word.

★

3. a. Listen as your teacher reads the Scripture that this play is taken from. (Luke 2:41-52)

b. After hearing the Scripture and the part of the play in our lesson, what do you think will happen next? What do you think Jesus' attitude will be about leaving the temple?

c. We all have earthly parents to love and obey. When we love and obey our earthly parents, it also pleases someone else. Whom does it please?

d. Together with your teacher, make a list of the things you do now that please your earthly parents. Remember, obeying our parents pleases our Heavenly Father, too.

e. Practice your spelling words in your Spelling Bee today.

---

b. The words the characters speak (lines).
(They cross the stage and seem to be looking in an open door.)

2.

c. Mary
(underlined in yellow) -
"Did you look in the temple?
Joseph, there he is sitting among all the teachers. Look how he is listening to them."

Joseph
(underlined in green) -
"No, I never thought to look there. It's just across the street. Let's go over there."

See page 289.

3.

b. Jesus went with Joseph and Mary. His attitude was one of obedience.

c. God

See page 289.

4. a. Read the following short play.

Optional Props: chair, jacket, bag, blanket, jar, container

A Visit to the Pond

Mother: (sitting in a chair) Well, it's almost time for spring.
Ann: (sitting by her mother) Yes, it's a wonderful, sunny day.
David: (jumps up and down in an excited way) Oh, Mother,
    let's walk down to the pond!
Mother: (stands up and looks out the window) Yes,
    children, you are right. It is a good day to be outside. We
    will go down to the pond.
Ann: Yea! (claps her hands and puts on her jacket)
David: I will bring bread to feed the ducks and fish.
    (holds up bag)
Ann: I will bring a jar to catch minnows. (holds up
    container)
Mother: I will bring a blanket to sit on. Come on, let's go.
    (They walk out together.)

4.
b. Self-explanatory

b. There are three characters in this play. Underline the name of
each character with these colors:

Mother	-	yellow
Ann	-	green
David	-	blue

Underline the stage directions for each character in red.

c. Self-explanatory

c. Now go back and underline the words spoken by each
character in their own color. (You may want to use
highlighter markers instead of crayons or colored pencils.)

d. Choose parts and read the play. You may want to gather the
items on the prop list before you begin.

e. Take your oral or written spelling pretest today.
                                 ★

See page 289.

5. a. Choose a familiar story to act out. The story can be acted out
as a play with people playing the parts, as a puppet show, or a
flannel board story. This can be as elaborate or as simple as
time and creativity allows. Some good stories to act out are

David and Goliath (without the stone throwing, of course), Noah's Ark (stuffed animals are great), Jesus calming the storm, etc. You can also choose well-known stories, such as "Little Red Riding Hood," "The Three Bears," etc. Any familiar story will do.

b. Gather the props that will help you tell the story. Choose the part or parts that each person will play.

c. Decide whether or not you will speak as part of your role, or just act it out as someone tells or reads the story.

d. Put on your play. Take turns playing different parts so you will know more about each character's role in the story.

e. Optional: Take your spelling test today.

pup

sun

fun

ten

men

tip

sit

rip

nut

hut

let

hem

set

him

fin

Review Activities

1. *Parts of a Play*
   Read this section of a play and answer the following questions.

Ryan:	(wiping his eyes) I can't find my puppy.
Jason:	(putting his arm around Ryan) Let's go look for him together.
Ryan:	I've already looked for him. (sobbing)
Jason:	We will keep trying until we find him.

   a. Who are the characters in the play?
   b. Circle the colon that follows each character's lines.
   c. Underline the stage directions.

1.
a. Ryan, Jason
b. self-explanatory
c. (wiping his eyes)
   (putting his arm
   around Ryan)
   (sobbing)

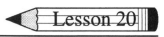

When John grew up, he did special work for God. John preached that everyone should be sorry for their sins and stop doing wrong. John told the people, "Jesus is coming soon."

Bible Stories to Read by Martha Rohrer.
Used by permission, Rod and Staff, Inc.
Crockett, Kentucky 41413

Bible Stories to Read by Martha Rohrer.
Used by permission, Rod and Staff, Inc.
Crockett, Kentucky 41413

1. a. Listen as your teacher reads the literature passage. Take the passage from dictation or copy the sentences. Compare your copy to the literature passage and make corrections.

   b. Copy the spelling words from *Focus on Spelling*. Say the words aloud as you write them. Some words spell the /**r**/ sound at the beginning of a word with **wr**.

   > ### Focus on Spelling
   > write   wrap   wreck   wrote   wrong
   > **Bonus Word:** special

2. a. Read the literature passage to your teacher. What did John say? With a blue pencil, underline the words spoken by John. The first word in a quotation always begins with a capital letter.

   b. Quotation marks (" ") are placed around the actual spoken words. With a blue pencil, circle the quotation marks in the literature passage.

   > **Punctuation Pointer**
   >
   > **Quotation marks** are placed around the actual spoken words.

   c. Look at the last sentence of the literature passage again. A comma (**,**) comes before the opening quotation mark. With a green pencil, circle this comma. What punctuation comes before the closing quotation mark?

✏ Teacher's Note:
As your student completes each lesson, choose skills from the *Review Activities* that he needs. The *Review Activities* follow each lesson.

✏ Teacher's Note:
When reading this literature passage to your student, stress your voice when speaking John's quotation.

At this time, just explain to your student that the words John spoke are enclosed with quotation marks. Show him the correct formation - " ". Quotations are taught in the next activity.

See page 289.

**2.
a. Jesus is coming soon.**

c. period

2.

d. 1) John said, "Stop doing wrong."

2) The people asked, "When is Jesus coming?"

3) John replied, "He is coming soon."

e. 1) Eric asked, "Why is tennis such a noisy sport?"

2) The boys replied, "We don't know."

3) Eric laughed, "Because everyone raises a racket!"

f.   Possible answer: Emily said, "I would like ice cream."

3.

a. John

d. Place quotation marks around the actual words spoken.

1) John said, Stop doing wrong.
2) The people asked, When is Jesus coming?
3) John replied, He is coming soon.

e. Remember that the first word of a quotation begins with a capital letter. Correct the following sentences by adding capitalization.

1) Eric asked, "why is tennis such a noisy sport?"
2) The boys replied, "we don't know."
3) Eric laughed, "because everyone raises a racket!"

Grammar Guide

Begin the first word of
a quotation with a **capital letter**.

---

f. Complete the following quotation.

Mother asked, "What would you like for dessert?"

   (Your name)   said, "_____."

g. Try writing your own quotation.

h. **SEE-SPELL-SAY:** Look and **see** each word on the spelling list. **Spell** each word aloud. **Say** the word.

3. a. There are two main parts of a sentence. The part that names what the sentence is about is called the subject. The part that tells something about the subject is called the predicate. A complete sentence usually has a subject and predicate. Look at the second sentence in our literature passage. Whom is

---

Grammar Guide

Complete sentence -
expresses a complete
thought

Grammar Guide

Subject - tells who or what
the sentence is about
Predicate - tells something
about the subject

---

the sentence about? In red, underline the word that tells whom the sentence is about. This word is the subject of the sentence.

b. The sentence is about John. What does the sentence tell us about John? In blue, underline the words that tell us what John did. This part of the sentence is called the predicate.

c. Look at the following sentence in your *Student Activity Book* or copy on paper or chalkboard.

The cat is black and white.

Underline in red, or point out, the words that name what the sentence is about. Underline in blue, or point out, the words that tell something about what was named.

d. Read each sentence. Underline the subject of the sentence in red. Underline the predicate, or part that tells about the subject, in blue.

1) My dog is jumping and barking.
2) Mother went to the store.
3) I like to eat ice cream.
4) The boat is floating in the water.
5) Bill can play with the toys.
6) Dad likes to go camping.

e. Practice your spelling words with your Spelling Bee today.

4. a. Usually when we want to show that something has already happened (past tense), we add **-ed** to the end of the word. Many words form the past tense by adding **-ed**.

Ex: Today, I clean.
     Yesterday, I cleaned.

Find the word in your literature passage that ends with **-ed**.

b. Some words show that something has already happened without adding **-ed**. A new word is used to show that something has already happened.

---

b. John <u>preached that everyone should be sorry for their sins and stop doing wrong.</u>

3.
c. red-cat
   blue-black, white

d. 1) Subject: - My dog,
      Predicate: - is jumping and barking
   2) Subject: - Mother
      Predicate: - went to the store
   3) Subject: - I
      Predicate: - like to eat ice cream
   4) Subject: - The boat
      Predicate: - is floating in the water
   5) Subject: - Bill
      Predicate: - can play with the toys
   6) Subject: - Dad
      Predicate: - likes to go camping

See page 289.

4. a.
✐ **Teacher's Note:**
These are called regular verbs.

preached

b. ✐ **Teacher's Note:**
These are called irregular verbs.

b. 1) grew
** 2) told**
** 3) did**

4.

c. talk - talked
** run   - ran**
** bake - baked**
** make - made**
** jump - jumped**
** smile - smiled**
** think - thought**

d. 1) baked
** 2) jumped**
** 3) ran**
** 4) smiled**
** 5) thought**
** 6) talked**
** 7) made**

f. Possible answers:
** Before John was born,**
** an angel told John's**
** father that many people**
** would be happy because**
** of John's birth. The**
** angel said that John**
** would be great in the**
** sight of the Lord. John**
** the Baptist was the man**
** of whom the prophet**
** Isaiah spoke in Isaiah**
** 40:3. Jesus asked John**
** to baptize him.**

Ex: Today, I write
    Yesterday, I wrote.

Find the words in your literature passage that may be used to complete these sentences.

1) Today, I grow.   Yesterday, I _____.
2) Today, I tell.   Yesterday, I _____.
3) Today, I do.   Yesterday, I _____.

c. Match each word with the correct word that shows it has already happened:

Today, I...	**Yesterday, I...**
talk	made
run	baked
bake	talked
make	jumped
jump	ran
smile	thought
think	smiled

d. Fill in the following blanks using the words in the box.

made	baked	talked	jumped
ran	thought	smiled	

1) We were hungry, so we _____ cookies.
2) The frog _____ out of the bucket.
3) The boy with the ball _____ for a touchdown.
4) I _____ at my new baby sister.
5) We came home because we _____ it was time for dinner.
6) When Grandma called on the phone, I _____ to her.
7) After I got up, I _____ my bed.

e. John is a very interesting person in the Bible. Listen as your teacher reads these Scriptures to you about John.

Luke 1:5-25; 57-80   Matthew 3:1-17

f. What special things happened to John, and how was he different from others? Write sentences that tell about John.

g. These sentences will make a paragraph. We always start the
first sentence of a paragraph differently, by indenting it, or
starting about an inch from the left margin. Choose a book
and let your teacher show you the beginning of a paragraph.

h. Optional: John had some unusual characteristics. Using the
Bible verses, draw a picture of what you think John looked
like, including where he lived and what he ate.

i. Take an oral written spelling pretest today.

5. a. A pronoun takes the place of a noun, or naming word.
It is a shorter way of writing so that you don't have to
keep repeating the name of a person or thing. Replace the
word(s) in italics with the correct pronoun in the box.

They	He	She	We	It

1) *Bill* went to the store. _____went to the store.
2) *Mother* washed the dishes. _____washed the dishes.
3) *Bill and Bob* played ball. _____ played ball.
4) *Sally and I* rode our bikes. _____ rode our bikes.
5) *The car* is in the road. _____ is in the road.

b. A pronoun we use often is the word *I*. The pronoun *I* is a way
of talking about yourself instead of using your name. If your
name is Bill, it would be funny for you to say, "Bill rode the
bike to the park." It would be better to say, "I rode the bike to
the park." Write three sentences about yourself beginning
with the word *I*.

c. Underline the pronouns used in each sentence:

1) They brought a cake for the party.
2) We are going to visit Grandma.
3) Please put it back.
4) She likes to grow flowers in the garden.
5) I got to help build the birdhouse.
6) The game will start when he comes.

5.
a. 1) He
   2) She
   3) They
   4) We
   5) It

c. 1) They
   2) We
   3) it
   4) She
   5) I
   6) he

d. Mom and I are very happy. *We* are going on a trip to the lake. We will go boating on *it*. Dad is coming, too. *He* likes to camp. Mom and Dad are happy to go on this trip. *They* are ready for a fun time. Mom is calling. *She* says it's time to go. Goodbye!

See page 290.

d. Rewrite this paragraph using pronouns for the italicized words. Remember to indent the first sentence.

    Mom and I are very happy. *Mom and I* are going on a trip to the lake. We will go boating on *the lake*. Dad is coming, too. *Dad* likes to camp. Mom and Dad are happy to go on this trip. *Mom and dad* are ready for a fun time. Mom is calling. *Mom* says it's time to go. Goodbye!

e. Optional: Take your spelling test today.

★

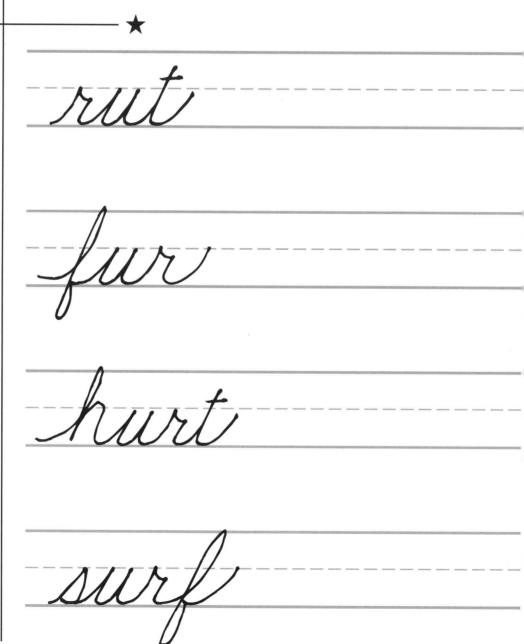

rut

fur

hurt

surf

twin

tent

rest

sell

nets

pens

hill

sits

lift

ring

tiny

Review Activities

1. *Quotation marks*
   Place quotation marks around the actual words spoken.

   a. Steve yelled, Look outside!
   b. Casey exclaimed, It's snowing!
   c. Mom asked, What's going on?

2. *Capitilization*
   Rewrite these sentences, adding capitalization.

   a. James asked, "may I have another cookie?"
   b. Mother replied, "you may have one more cookie."

3. *Subject / Predicate*
   Circle the subject and underline the predicate.

   a. The boy chased the dog.
   b. The big dog ran under the fence.
   c. The cat climbed a tall tree.
   d. The kitten hid in the bushes.

4. *Past Tense*
   Match the verb on the left to the verb on the right that shows it has already happened.

   a. talk   made
   b. think   ran
   c. make   smiled
   d. smile   talked
   e. run   thought

5. *Pronouns*
   Rewrite the sentences, replacing the nouns with the correct pronoun.

   a. *Sandy and Eric* came to my house.
   b. *Sara, Eric, and I* played bingo.
   c. *Sara* won the game.
   d. *The game* was fun.

1.
a. Steve yelled, "Look outside!"
b. Casey exclaimed, "It's snowing!"
c. Mom asked, "What's going on?"

2.
a. James asked, "May I have another cookie?"
b. Mother replied, "You may have one more cookie."

3.
a. (The boy) chased the dog.
b. (The big dog) ran under the fence.
c. (The cat) climbed a tall tree.
d. (The kitten) hid in the bushes.

4.
a. talk - talked
b. think - thought
c. make - made
d. smile - smiled
e. run   - ran

5.
a. They
b. We
c. She
d. It

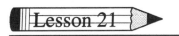

John baptized people in the Jordan River. One day Jesus came to John. Jesus wanted to please God so He asked John to baptize Him. John baptized Jesus in the Jordan River.

Bible Stories to Read by Martha Rohrer. Used by permission, Rod and Staff, Inc. Crockett, Kentucky 41413

Teacher's Note: As your student completes each lesson, choose skills from the *Review Activities* that he needs. The *Review Activities* follow each lesson.

See page 290.

2.

a. **Teacher's Note:** You may read the sentences if your student needs it to understand the word given.

b. **Teacher's Note:** Read the following sentences to your student to be written from dictation. Read slowly, repeating it several times. Encourage your student to just listen the first time, and then begin. Do not be concerned about saying it too often. The goal is for your student to be able to write the sentences. Speed and accuracy will be increased over time.

c. **Teacher's Note:** After your student's first attempt, show him how to correct any mistakes. Read the sentence again, several times if needed. Repeat the correction process. Make sure to praise improvements. He may attempt it a third time if he desires; however, be alert to fatigue. If your student is overly tired or discouraged at this point, it is best to end the session, highlighting improvements.

1. a. Listen as your teacher reads the literature passage. Write these sentences from dictation the second time she reads them, or copy them. Compare your copy to the literature passage and make corrections.

   b. Review the spelling lists in Lessons 15, 17, 19, and 20.

2. a. Either orally or in writing, spell the following words for your teacher.

   1) pleasing A windchime gives a *pleasing* sound.
   2) wreck   He was in a car *wreck* but was not hurt.
   3) write   I will *write* my name.
   4) where   *Where* is my pencil?
   5) thought   After I *thought* about it, I made my decision.
   6) why   *Why* is today a special day?
   7) fought   David *fought* Goliath.
   8) grow   Mother will *grow* flowers in her garden.

   b. Listen to your teacher as she dictates these sentences to you.

   1) The teacher brought the wrong one.
   2) I am pleased to write a special note.

   c. After your teacher has checked your sentences, make any corrections.

   Cover your paper so that you can not see your corrected sentence. Listen again to your teacher as she dictates the same sentences again. Repeat the correction process.

3. a. There are three sounds that **-ed** can make at the end of a word:

    1) **/ed/** like in the word, _pointed_
    2) **/t/** like in the word, _boxed_
    3) **/d/** like in the word, _yelled_

See page 290.

> **Phonics Fact**
>
> **-ed** at the end of a word can say /ed/ as in _pointed_, /t/ as in _boxed_, and /d/ as in _yelled_

Read the following words for your teacher and listen to the ending sound.

painted	waited	boxed
baked	yelled	dried

b. Circle the word in the literature passage where the **-ed** at the end says **/t/**, as in, _baked_. Underline the word in your sentences where the **-ed** at the end says **/d/**, as in, _yelled_. Draw a box around the word in your sentences where the **-ed** at the end says **/ed/**, as in, _painted_.

c. Read the following list of words to your teacher. Use the page provided in the _Student Activity Book_ for this activity, or make three columns with the headings **/t/**, **/d/**, and **/ed/**. Write each word under the correct column which tells the sound **-ed** makes:

seated	mixed	waved
backed	followed	grounded
ended	benched	cleaned
stayed	graded	cracked
needed	passed	called

d. Choose one word from each column and make up a sentence using that word. You may do this orally or in writing.

3.

b. (asked)
  baptized
  [wanted]

c.

/ed/	/d/
seated	waved
grounded	followed
ended	cleaned
graded	stayed
needed	called

/t/
mixed
backed
benched
cracked
passed

4.

a. repent - to feel sorry for one's ways and then to change

b. John preached that everyone should be sorry for their sins and stop doing wrong.

   everyone

c. baptize - to publicly show that you have decided to follow Jesus

See page 290.

✏ **Teacher's Note:**
Remind your student of any needed pronunciations during reading.

See page 290.

4. a. The word *repent* is a very important word for those who believe in Jesus. Look up the word *repent* in the dictionary. Write the word and its meaning in your own words.

   b. Find the sentence in the literature passage in Lesson 20 that shows John telling the people to repent. Read this sentence to your teacher. Who does John say needs to repent?

   c. There is another important word in our literature passage for those who believe in Jesus. This word is *baptize*. Look up the word *baptize* in the dictionary. Write the word and its meaning in your own words.

   d. Discuss with your teacher what the words *repent* and *baptize* mean. Discuss what your family believes about baptism. Have you ever been baptized? If you have, tell your teacher what you think that means.

★

5. a. Listen as your teacher reads the vocabulary for this story.

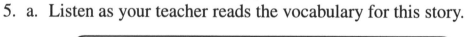

Vocabulary			
arrive	finally	excited	surround
reflection	bass	bait	bream wonder

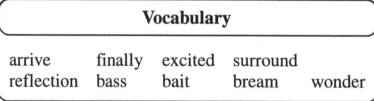

   b. Read the story to your teacher.

★

Gone Fishing

When I was a young boy, my family lived with another family in a big house in the city. Our families had fun times together, and I had fun with a little girl in the other family named Michelle. Michelle and I were best friends.

One day, my mother told me that Michelle and her family were moving away. They were moving to the country. My mother said that I wouldn't be able to see the family very much anymore. I was very sad, but Michelle told me that I would be able to come and visit her family in the summer.

That year it felt as if summer would never arrive. When it finally came, I was so excited. I was going to spend a whole week in the country with my best friend. It was a long drive, but it was worth it to see Michelle and her new home. She lived on a lake surrounded by tall pine trees. Being from the city, I had never seen such a pretty blue lake, with tall grass growing around the banks. The water was so clear and blue, and the sun made a sparkling reflection dance across the water. As Michelle and I peered down into the water from her dock, we could see large bass swimming slowly around the grass at the bottom of the lake.

Michelle's father had just bought her and her sisters fishing poles, so we decided to go fishing that afternoon. All we had for bait was pieces of bread, but we knew we would have fun even if we didn't catch anything. But as soon as we tossed in our hooks, little bream (a small freshwater fish) began to attack our bait. We both sat with wide-eyed wonder at the dozens of little fish that seemed to have come from out of nowhere! Soon, as often happens on hot summer afternoons, it started to rain. It began to rain so hard we could hardly see. So, we sat there, Michelle and I, laughing at the rain and smiling at the fish.

That day Michelle and I became even better friends. We were given a memory that kept our friendship together, even though we could not be together anymore. It's a fishing trip that has become stuck in my mind. I can still remember that clear blue lake, even though it has long since dried up, and I can still remember my smiling friend, even though she has moved away. Looking back, I think perhaps it was our happiness that made that lake so blue and beautiful.

5.

b. 1) They lived in a big house in the city.

2) The family moved away and this made the child in the story very sad.

3) She said that her friend could come and visit her over the summer.

4) Her family lived on a clear blue lake with pine trees all around.

5) They went fishing.

6) It began to rain.

7) The author says it looked so blue because those two children were so happy.

Discussion Questions:

1) Where did the two families live together?
2) What happened to Michelle and her family? How did this make the child feel?
3) What did Michelle tell her friend before she left?
4) Describe Michelle's new home.
5) What did Michelle and her friend do together?
6) What happened as they were fishing?
7) What does the author say about why the lake looked so blue?

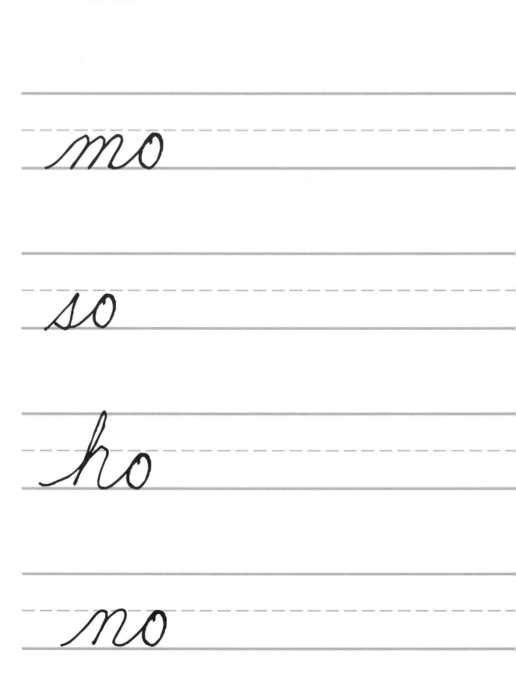

to

ma

pa

la

ha

ta

ac

ic

uc

ec

Review Activities

Choose the skills your student needs to review.

1. *Suffix -ed*
   Add the suffix **-ed** to these words. Say the words aloud and decide if the word says **/t/**, **/d/**, or **/ed/**.

   a. lift
   b. yell
   c. jump
   d. play
   e. point
   f. fix

1.
a. lifted /ed/
b. yelled /d/
c. jumped /t/
d. played /d/
e. pointed /ed/
f. fixed /t/

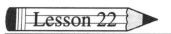

When they came up out of the water, God's Spirit came down from heaven like a dove and sat upon Jesus. Also a voice from heaven said, "This is my beloved Son, in whom I am well pleased."

Bible Stories to Read by Martha Rohrer.
Used by permission, Rod and Staff, Inc.
Crockett, Kentucky 41413

1. **Teacher's Note:**
When reading the literature passage to your student, remind your student of the actual words spoken.

See page 290.

2. b. **Teacher's Note:**
You may give sentences if your student needs them to understand the word given.

c. **Teacher's Note:**
Read the following sentences to your student to be written from dictation. Read slowly, repeating it several times. Encourage your student to just listen the first time, and then begin. Do not be concerned about saying it too often. The goal is for your student to be able to write the sentences. Speed and accuracy will be increased over time.

2. d. **Teacher's Note:**
After your student's first attempt, show him how to correct any mistakes. Read the sentence again, several times if needed. Repeat the correction process. Make sure to praise improvements. He may attempt it a third time if he desires; however, be alert to fatigue. If your student is overly tired or discouraged at this point, it is best to end the session, highlighting improvements.

1. Listen as your teacher reads the literature passage. Write these sentence from dictation the second time she reads them, or copy the sentences. Compare your copy to the literature passage and make corrections.

★

2. a. Review the spelling lists in Lessons 1 - 20.

   b. Spell the following words for your teacher.

      1) knife   My father will teach me how to use a *knife*.
      2) wrote   I *wrote* a letter today.
      3) everything   Sometimes, *everything* goes right.
      4) when   *When* are you coming?
      5) who   *Who* is coming?
      6) group   Our team posed for a *group* picture.
      7) leave   Do not *leave* without your jacket.
      8) wear   I will *wear* my red shirt.
      9) sometimes   *Sometimes* I forget my manners.
      10) first   He came *first* in the race.
      11) clear   The sky will *clear* after the rain.
      12) raise   I will *raise* the blinds.
      13) grow   I will *grow* a garden.
      14) brought   She *brought* her dog.
      15) wrong   This is the *wrong* book.

   c. Listen to your teacher as she dictates sentences to you.

      1) The girl will know when everybody is at the beach.
      2) You will be pleased to leave tomorrow.

   d. After your teacher has checked your sentences, make any corrections. Cover your paper so that you can not see your corrected sentence. Listen again to your teacher as she

dictates the same sentence again. Repeat the correction
process.

See page 290.

★ ────────────────────────

a. Often we want to show that something has already happened
(past tense), so we often add the suffix **-ed** to the end of
the word.

Ex: Today, I *cook* the meal.
     Yesterday, I *cooked* the meal.

Find two words in your literature passage that end with the
suffix **-ed**. Write each word. Tell your teacher what
happened to the silent **e** when you added **-ed**.

3. a. ✏ **Teacher's Note:**
These words are called
regular verbs.

beloved, pleased
The silent e was dropped.

b. There are three words in our literature passage that show
something has already happened. They do not show it with
-ed added to the end, but the spelling of the word changes.
Find the words in our literature passage to fill in the blanks.

1) Today, I *come*. Yesterday, I _____.
2) Today, I *sit*. Yesterday, I _____.
3) Today, I *say*. Yesterday, I _____.

b. ✏ **Teacher's Note:**
These words are called
irregular verbs.

1) came
2) sat
3) said

c. Match these words with the words that show it has already
happened.

Today, I...	**Yesterday, I...**
feel	told
pay	took
begin	ate
keep	felt
tell	found
take	began
find	paid
eat	kept

c. feel   - felt
pay   - paid
begin - began
keep   - kept
tell   - told
take   - took
find   - found
eat   - ate

d. Fill in the following blanks using the words in the box.

told	took	ate	felt
began	paid	kept	found

d. 1) found
   2) began
   3) paid
   4) ate
   5) told
   6) kept
   7) took
   8) felt

4.
a. This is my beloved Son, in whom I am well pleased.
b. quotation marks

d. capital letter

e. 1) Jamie asked his friends, "What has eight wheels and flies?"
   2) His friends relied, "We don't know."
   3) Jamie said, "A garbage truck!"

f. 1) Cindy asked, "What is black and white and read (red) all over?"
   2) The girls replied, "We don't know."
   3) Cindy answered, "A sunburnt zebra!"

---

1) The boys _____ an old baseball in the dirt.
2) We _____ school in the fall.
3) After I washed his car, Mr. Smith _____ me.
4) When the cake was baked, we _____ a big piece.
5) Dad _____ us not to play near the street.
6) My dad _____ all his old baseball cards.
7) During the summer, my family _____ a trip.
8) Mom _____ tired after a long day of work.

4. a. Read the literature passage to your teacher. With a blue pencil, underline the words the voice from heaven spoke.

  b. What marks helped you know the words spoken?

  c. Read the literature passage again, using a different voice for the "voice from heaven."

  d. Look at the first word of the quotation which you underlined. What kind of letter begins the first word in a quotation?

  e. Review the *Punctuation Pointer* on quotation marks in Lesson 20.

    Add quotation marks around the actual words spoken.

    1) Jamie asked his friends, What has eight wheels and flies?
    2) His friends replied, We don't know.
    3) Jamie said, A garbage truck!

  f. Review the *Grammar Guide* on capitalization in quotations in Lesson 20.

    Add capitalization to the following quotations.

    1) Cindy asked, "what is black and white and read (red) all over?"
    2) The girls replied, "we don't know."
    3) Cindy answered, "a sunburnt zebra."

  g. Today, you are going to learn about **facts** and **opinions**. Listen to your teacher as she reads the following paragraph.

The Tropical Fish Store has many different kinds of sea creatures. They have thirty separate tanks with colorful tropical fish. The fish store has fish of all shapes, sizes, and colors. In the back of the store, there are ten tanks with giant lobsters and crabs. The store even sells small octopuses and squid. The Tropical Fish Store also sells supplies and food for all the fish and other creatures they carry. You can buy aquariums and food for the tiniest guppy to the largest lobster.

h. After reading the paragraph with your teacher, think about the facts you have learned about the Tropical Fish Store. Now, decide whether or not the following statements are facts (things that are true) or opinions (what someone thinks).

Write **F** for Fact or **O** for Opinion on the line in front of each statement.

1) ___ The Tropical Fish Store carries many different kinds of fish.
2) ___ The Tropical Fish Store sells more than just fish.
3) ___ The Tropical Fish Store is a fun place to visit.
4) ___ The fish at the Tropical Fish Store are the prettiest fish in town.
5) ___ The Tropical Fish Store can supply you with food and aquariums for any creature you buy at the store.

5. a. Our literature passage about Jesus' baptism paints a beautiful picture of baptism and of God showing His love and pleasure with His Son. Discuss with your teacher how the Scripture (Luke 3:21-22) describes Jesus' baptism.

b. Draw a picture of what you think His baptism was like or what any other baptism would look like.

c. Why do you think Jesus was baptized? Do you think He needed to be baptized? Discuss this question with your teacher, and write your answer on the back of your picture.

4.
h. 1) F
  2) F
  3) O
  4) O
  5) F

5.
c. Allow for discussion.

See page 290.

★

ad

ed

id

ud

sad

mud

ag

eg

ig

rig

rag

fig

aq

iq

eq

uq

Review Activities

1. *Suffix -ed*
Add the suffix **-ed** to these words.

   a. show
   b. lift
   c. pour
   d. look

2. *Past tense*
Match the verb on the left to the verb on the right that shows it has already happened.

   a. feel   told
   b. keep   took
   c. pay   kept
   d. tell   paid
   e. take   felt

3. *Quotations*
Underline the actual words spoken.

Tom said, "I will be late today."

4. *Facts and Opinions*

   a. Write a sentence about yourself stating a fact.
   b. Write a sentence about yourself stating an opinion.

1.
a. showed
b. lifted
c. poured
d. looked

2.
a. feel   -   felt
b. keep   -   kept
c. pay   -   paid
d. tell   -   told
e. take   -   took

3.
Tom said, "<u>I will be late today</u>."

4. Answers will vary. Possible example:
a. I am nine years old.
b. My baseball team is the best team.

Assessment 5
(Lessons 19 - 22)

1.

"I like to play ball,"
said Jim.

1. Add quotation marks and capitalization.

   I like to play ball said jim.

2.
a. played
b. worked
c. filled
d. wished

2. Write the past tense for these verbs. Show that the action has already happened.

   a. play
   b. work
   c. fill
   d. wish

3.
a. took
b. kept
c. began
d. found

3. Write the past tense for these verbs. Show that the action has already happened.

   a. take
   b. keep
   c. begin
   d. find

4.
a. opinion
b. fact

4. Write the word *fact* or *opinion* in the blanks.

   a. A statement that tells what someone feels about something is called a(n) _____.
   b. A statement that tells something true is called a(n) _____.

Literature Link

Literature Link

1. There are two reading options for this lesson:

   Option 1 - Find the book, *The Courage of Sarah Noble*, by Alice Dalgliesh. Read half of the story today.

Summary
The Courage of Sarah Noble

Sarah Noble is an eight-year-old girl who travels with her father from their home in the Massachusetts colony to the site of their new homeland in New Milford, Connecticut. The year is 1707, and many colonists are moving west.

After their journey, Sarah and her father start to settle the land. Indians become their friends, and in the fall, the house is finished. Now comes the greatest challenge of all. Father must return to get the rest of the family. What is Sarah to do? Sarah must prove that she has courage.

Option 2 - Read the story, "Young Daniel - Boy of the Woods." You will have time tomorrow to finish the story. Read the vocabulary words with your teacher.

Vocabulary		
pioneer	Pennsylvania	Squire
Sarah	special	plowing
bareback	tomahawk	respect

The Courage of Sarah Noble
by Alice Dalgliesh Published
by Simon & Schuster

✐ Teacher's Note:
Remind your student of
any pronunciations
during reading.

Young Daniel - Boy of the Woods

Being a part of a pioneer family was exciting. It is true that life was very hard. It is also true that there was always something new happening. Growing up during the 1730's was never dull.

Daniel Boone was born in 1734 in Pennsylvania. The Boone family lived on a farm. His father's name was Squire. His mother's name was Sarah. There were eleven children in the Boone family.

Just like most other pioneer boys, Daniel grew up learning many things. His mother wanted him to learn from books, but Daniel wanted to learn the ways of the woods. He always tried to get away when it was time to read or write or spell. He was not very good at these things. He was very good at *other* things.

What Daniel loved to learn most about was the forest, the animals, how to track, and how to hide. These skills would keep him safe. He had a special love for animals. He watched them and learned about them.

Daniel also had to do the work of a pioneer boy. By the time he was ten, he chopped wood and helped with the plowing. He helped take care of the animals and hitch up the horses. He milked the cows and helped make butter. He helped pick berries when they were ripe and gather nuts before winter came. There was always work to do. The work made Daniel strong.

Daniel learned about Indians, too. He could do many things like the Indians. He could ride a horse bareback (without a saddle). He could throw a tomahawk. He could walk without making a sound. He learned how to get along with Indians, too. They were very proud, and Daniel learned how to treat them with respect.

When Daniel was twelve years old, he was given a special present by his father — his first gun! He was so excited! He could now hunt like his brothers. Now, Daniel was ready to live by himself in the woods. He could take care of himself. Sometimes, he would hunt for days or weeks. This was hard for his mother. But soon she understood that Daniel's life would be spent in the forests.

Daniel Boone grew up to be a great man. He helped many people find new places to make their homes. He helped make new roads in the forests. The little pioneer boy from Pennsylvania helped our new country grow. The things Daniel learned about the forests and animals helped us all.

2. a. Continue the book or story from yesterday. When it is completed, discuss it with your teacher, using the following questions:

Discussion Questions for *The Courage of Sarah Noble*:

1) Why was Sarah making the journey to New Milford with her father?
2) What was her mother's advice to her as she left?
3) What did the Robinson children tell her about Indians?
4) What book did Sarah bring with her to read?
5) How did Sarah first meet the Indians? Did they become friends?
6) What was Sarah to do while her father went to get the family?
7) How did Sarah like staying with Tall John? What was different for Sarah?
8) How did Sarah feel when her family arrived? How did Sarah feel about herself after they arrived?

---

2. a. *The Courage of Sarah Noble*

1) They were going to build a house.
2) "Keep up your courage," her mother had told her.
3) They told her that the Indians will kill her and eat her and do all sorts of awful things to her. But Abigail told Sarah that the boys are only teasing.
4) The Bible
5) The little Indian children came up to her while she was reading the Bible. Eventually, they lost their fear of her just as she lost her fear of them. They became friends.
6) She stayed with Tall John and his family.
7) At first she was sad and afraid, but she soon felt more comfortable with the Indian family. Sarah wore different clothes and shoes than she used to. She helped the Indian women with their jobs also.
8) She could hardly wait to see them. She was very excited to see her family. She felt that she was nearly a woman.

Discussion Questions for "Young Daniel - Boy of the Woods":

1) Did Daniel grow up in a big family?
2) Did Daniel like learning things from books? Who wanted him to learn from books?
3) What did Daniel love to learn about? What was his special love?
4) Name some of Daniel's chores.
5) What could Daniel do as well as an Indian?
6) What special gift was Daniel given when he became twelve years old?
7) What did Daniel want to do most of all?
8) How did Daniel's interests as a child help us as a country?

b. The stories of Sarah Noble and Daniel Boone tell about the lives of pioneer children. Both these children lived in the early 1700's. Their lives were very different from the children of today. After talking with your teacher, make a list of five things that pioneer children had to do each day. Include any regular chores you think they might have done.

c. Now think about what you do each day. Make a list of five things you might do each day. Include any regular chores you do. Look at the two lists and find things that are the same. Now, look at the two lists and find things that are different.

d. Now make a list of things you think pioneer children may have done for fun. Look at your list. Are any of their activities things you would like to do today?

e. Children in pioneer days didn't have much time for play. They had to do many chores to help their families. Doing chores made them strong and healthy. It also was a help to their families. Talk with your teacher about the things you can do around your house that would help your family. If you already do chores to help out, see if there are any chores you could improve. Together with your teacher, make a daily chore list (if you don't have one). Mark every day that you do each chore. Helping out makes you feel good about being part of a family.

2. a. "Young Daniel"
   1) Yes, there were eleven children in his family.
   2) No. His mother especially wanted him to learn from books.
   3) He was good at learning about the ways of the woods and animals and hunting and tracking. He had a special love for animals.
   4) Daniel would chop wood, help with plowing, take care of the family's animals, milk cows, make butter, and gather nuts and berries.
   5) He could ride bareback, throw a tomahawk and walk without a sound, just like his Indian friends.
   6) His first gun
   7) He wanted to hunt and live in the woods most of all.
   8) Daniel helped people to find new places to build their homes, made new roads in the forests, and helped our country to grow.

b. Possible Answers
   chop wood, milk cows, help with animals, sew, cook keep younger children, hunt, fish, etc.

3. a. Since the pioneer life was so hard, you can be grateful to those pioneers who helped our country grow. With your teacher, look at this list of names. Choose one or two names. Use an encyclopedia or library books to read about these people.

   Daniel Boone   Davy Crockett
   Marcus Whitman   Zebulon Pike
   Narcissa Whitman   Lewis and Clark

   b. Make a simple timeline of one of the pioneers you read about. Include pictures if you can. Include major events and pictures if you can.
   Ex:

   Born 1801   Died 1873

4.   After reading about these individuals, choose a way to present the information. You may draw a picture or write a paragraph. Prepare for this presentation.

5. a. Look up the words *bravery* and *courage* in the dictionary. These words have similar meanings and are called synonyms. Tell your teacher what these two words mean. Write a definition.

   b. Using the story of Sarah Noble or Daniel Boone, give an example of how they showed courage or bravery.

   c. Talk with your teacher about any of the following Bible characters. Discuss the ways they showed courage or bravery.

   Queen Esther (Book of Esther)   Joshua (Book of Joshua)
   David (as a boy; I Samuel)   Paul (The Apostle)

   d. Has there ever been a time in your life when you or someone in your family had to act bravely? Talk with your teacher about this. With your teacher, write several sentences telling about what happened and why you think it was brave.

I **C.A.N.** Assessment
for the
Literature Link on Frontier Life

After the *Literature Link* is completed, check off each I **C.A.N.** objective with your teacher.

C   I can **complete** my work.
     I can be **creative**.

A   I can be **accurate**.
     I can do my work with a good **attitude**.

N   I can do my work **neatly**.

This page may be photocopied for student's use.

EVERYDAY WORDS

New Skills

Describing Sentence	Fiction and Nonfiction
Lists	Predicting Outcome
Verse	Alphabetical Order
Adjective	Choral Reading
Adverb	Poetry
Article	Encyclopedia
Good/Well	Titles of Books

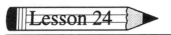

Teacher's Note:
As your student completes each lesson, choose skills from the *Review Activities* that he needs. The *Review Activities* follow each lesson.

Teacher's Note:
If you choose to dictate, tell your student when to begin a new line. Also, tell him that in this poem, the first word in each line is capitalized.

See page 290.

2.
a. bright, beautiful, great, small, wise, wonderful

Teacher's Note:
The word *all* can be used as an adjective; however, we will focus on the other adjectives in our sentences.

All things bright and beautiful,
All creatures, great and small,
All things wise and wonderful,
The Lord God made them all.

"The Creation" by Cecil Frances Alexander

1. a. Listen as your teacher reads the poem. Write the poem from dictation the second time she reads it, or copy it. Compare your copy to the literature passage and make corrections.

   b. Copy the spelling words from *Focus on Spelling*. Say the words aloud as you write them. Some words spell the /ī/ sound with **igh**.

   ### Focus on Spelling

   right   bright   light   night   might
   Bonus Word: wonderful

   ---

2. a. Describing words tell about people, places, and things. Describing words are called adjectives. There are six words in our sentences that tell about the things and creatures that God made. Underline each describing word.

   b. Using a dictionary, look up the meanings of the adjectives you have underlined. On a separate piece of paper write a brief definition for each adjective.

   c. The best way to add a new word to our vocabulary is to use it. Use three pieces of plain white paper and fold them in half. At the top of each section, write one of the adjectives you underlined. In each section, write the names of people, places, or things that the adjective you wrote at the top could describe. Think of as many examples for each adjective as you can.

   Ex: small - child, mouse, insect

d. Choose one word from each section. Make up a sentence using the adjective and the noun it is describing.

   Ex: An owl is wise.

e. **SEE-SPELL-SAY:** Look and **see** each word in the spelling list. **Spell** each word aloud. **Say** the word.

3. a. We can add a suffix, or additional letters, to the end of a word to change the meaning. A suffix is added to the end of the main word, called the base or root word. Using a red crayon or pencil, circle the word that has *wonder* as a base, or root, word.

   b. What suffix, or extra letters, has been added to this word? What do you think that suffix means? Tell your teacher what you think *wonderful* means. Use this word orally in a sentence.

   c. Here are some base or root words. Add the suffix **-ful** to the end of each base word.

      1) play   4) joy
      2) pain   5) color
      3) thank   6) prayer

   d. In the literature passage, find the word that has *beauty* as a base word. When you add the suffix **-ful** to the end of this word, the spelling changes. What change was made in the spelling? What rule can you think of that applies to consonant **y** at the end of a word when adding the suffix **-ful**?

   e. Practice your spelling words in your Spelling Bee today.

4. a. Our poem describes things and creatures that the Lord God made. Make a list of your favorite things and creatures.

   ★

   b. Either by cutting pictures out of magazines or by drawing, make pictures of some of your favorite things or creatures. Pictures may be used to express one's thoughts. Write the name of the thing or creature below each picture.

3.
a. wonderful

b. -ful, full of

   full of wonder
   or very good

c. 1) playful
   2) painful
   3) thankful
   4) joyful
   5) colorful
   6) prayerful

d. beautiful
   The *y* was changed to *i*.
   You change the *y* to *i* and
   add the suffix *-ful*.

✎ **Teacher's Note:**
When adding a suffix to a
word ending in *-y*, change
the *y* to *i*. If the *y* is
preceded by a vowel, then
leave the *y* and add the
suffix. The exception
to this rule is the suffix
-ing. When adding the
suffix *-ing* to a word ending
in *-y*, the *y* remains and you
just add *-ing*.

See page 290.

See page 290.

c. Make up a verse using three of your pictures. Start each line with a capital letter and end it with a comma (**,**). Add a fourth line that says, *The Lord God made them all.* Start the fourth line with a capital letter and end it with a period. This is called a verse.

d. Take your oral or written spelling pretest today.
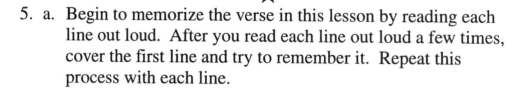

5. a. Begin to memorize the verse in this lesson by reading each line out loud. After you read each line out loud a few times, cover the first line and try to remember it. Repeat this process with each line.

b. You may want to practice holding up your pictures of creatures and things while you say the lines of the verse. Hold the pictures so that your audience can see them.

c. Review the poem in Lessons 10 - 13. Reread the verses and look at the pictures you made to present the poem to a group.

d. Presenting a poem to other people can be fun. After review, present the poem in Lessons 10 - 13 to a group of people or your family. It will be easier since you have already done this before.

e. Take your spelling test today.

See page 290.

oa

os

od

ob

og

om

or

oe

ou

of

oh

roast

coat

float

most

soft

Review Activities

1. *Possible answers.*
a. **fierce, mean**
b. **rainy, sunny**
c. **shiny, new**
d. **happy, friendly**

2.
a. **helpful**
b. **hopeful**
c. **restful**
d. **joyful**

1. *Adjectives*
Think of a describing word, or adjective, that can describe these words.

   a. tiger
   b. day
   c. car
   d. girls

2. *Suffix -ful*
Add the suffix **-ful** to these words and write the new words.

   a. help
   b. hope
   c. rest
   d. joy

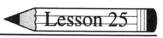

The purple-headed mountain,
The river running by,
The sunset and the morning
That brightens up the sky.

"The Creation" by Cecil Frances Alexander

1. a. Listen as your teacher reads the poem. Write the poem from dictation the second time she reads it, or copy it. Compare your copy to the literature passage and make corrections.

   b. Copy the spelling words from *Focus on Spelling*. Say the words aloud as you write them.

Focus on Spelling

morning   evening   sunrise   sunset   sunshine
Bonus Word: Sunday

---

2. a. Words that name people, places, and things are called nouns. Using a red pencil, underline only the words that tell the names of things and places in the literature passage.

   b. A small word comes before each one of our nouns. What word is it? The word *the* tells us a noun, or naming word, is coming. This is called an article. Circle the word *the* every time you see it in our sentences. Read the words you circled to your teacher, then tell her what noun comes after it. The words *a* and *an* are also articles.

   c. In the first line of our poem, there are some words between the word *the* and the word *mountain*. Underline these words in blue. These words are adjectives, or words that describe *mountain*.

✎ **Teacher's Note:**
As your student completes each lesson, choose skills from the *Review Activities* that he needs. The *Review Activities* follow each lesson.

✎ **Teacher's Note:**
If you choose to dictate, tell your student when to begin a new line. Also, tell him that in this poem, the first word in each line is capitalized.

See page 291.

2.

a. **mountain, river, sunset, morning, sky**

b. <u>the</u> mountain,
   <u>the</u> river, <u>the</u> sunset,
   <u>the</u> morning, <u>the</u> sky

✎ **Teacher's Note:**
Sometimes, as in "the purple-headed mountain," adjectives will precede the noun.

c. **purple-headed**

2.

d. 1) The fat black cat is
   playing.

2) Where do you want
   the new bike?

3) The clock says it's
   time for lunch.

4) Mother wants the
   blue plate for the
   meat.

5) When is the
   big game?

6) The book I like is
   on the brown table.

3.

a. no, no
   The author could be
   trying to convey that
   Creation is alive.

d. Read the following sentences to your teacher. Circle the article *the* in each sentence. Underline the noun which comes after the article. Draw an arrow from any adjective to the noun. Look carefully; there may be more than one article in a sentence.

> **Grammar Guide**
>
> **Article** - a small word that tells you a noun is coming
>
> *a   an   the*

Ex: The little white dog ran quickly.

1) The fat black cat is playing.
2) Where do you want the new bike?
3) The clock says it's time for lunch.
4) Mother wants the blue plate for the meat.
5) When is the big game?
6) The book I like is on the brown table.

e. **SEE-SPELL-SAY:** Look and **see** each word on the spelling list. **Spell** each word aloud. **Say** the word.

3. a. Read the first line of poetry aloud to your teacher. Do mountains really have purple heads? Read the second line aloud to your teacher. Does a river run by like a person? What do you think the author is telling us with these descriptions? Do they help you imagine what the mountains and river look like?

b. Either by drawing or choosing pictures from a magazine, show what you think these sentences describe. Make more than one picture.

c. On the back of each picture, write the sentence from the poem that describes it.

d. Can you think of another sentence to describe each picture, other than just the one used in the poem? Write another sentence on the back of each picture using your own words to describe it.

e. Practice your spelling words with your Spelling Bee today.

★

See page 291.

a. Practice taking turns reading the parts in this **choral reading**.
    After reading it one or two times, trade parts.

Girls or Person 1:   Summer is coming.
Boys or Person 2:   I can't wait!
Girls or Person 1:   It will soon be warming.
Boys or Person 2:   I can't wait!
Girls or Person 1:   Time for swimming.
Boys or Person 2:   I can't wait!
All Together: Summer is here!

b. Can you think of movements that can be done with this choral
    reading? Perhaps you would like to use props with this
    choral reading, such as hats or towels. On the last line,
    everyone could put on sunglasses. Be creative and then
    present this to a group.

c. Along with another person, take turns reading the lines of the
    poem aloud. Read the last line together aloud. Practice
    reading the poem this way until you memorize it. Do the
    same thing with each verse.

d. Take your spelling pretest today.

★

See page 291.

5. a. Use the words in the box from Lessons 24 - 25 to fill in the blanks of the following crossword puzzle. Remember, one letter to a box. If a letter is already in a box, don't write it again; just go on to the next letter in the word.

bright	mountain	sunset	wonderful
great	river	creatures	morning

DOWN:
1) when the sun goes down
2) All _____, great and small
3) A large stream is called a _____.
4) when you wake up

ACROSS:
5) a very tall part of the land
6) All things _____ and beautiful
7) Something that is very good is _____.
8) rhymes with *crate*

5.
a.

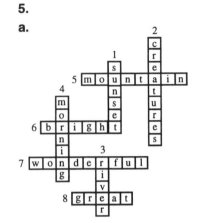

b. Take your spelling test today.

be

bu

br

bl

brag

bike

bus

born

ball

black

Review Activities

1. *Articles*
   Circle the articles and underline the nouns.

   a. a bear
   b. the horse
   c. an eel
   d. a donkey

2. *Adjectives and Nouns*
   Underline the nouns. Draw an arrow from the adjective to the noun it describes.

   a. The pretty bird flew away.
   b. The colorful rainbow shone brightly.
   c. The goat ate the old hat.
   d. The dog ran over the pretty flowers.

1.
a. (a) bear
b. (the) horse
c. (an) eel
d. (a) donkey

2.
a. The pretty bird flew away.
b. The colorful rainbow shone brightly.
c. The goat ate the old hat.
d. The dog ran over the pretty flowers.

The cold wind in the winter,
The pleasant summer sun,
The ripe fruits in the garden,
He made them every one.

"The Creation" by Cecil Frances Alexander

1. a. Listen as your teacher reads the poem. Write the poem from dictation the second time she reads it, or copy it. Compare your copy to the literature passage and make corrections.

   b. Copy the spelling words from *Focus on Spelling*. Say the words aloud as you write them.

Focus on Spelling

winter   summer   spring   garden   season
Bonus Word: fruit

---

2. a. Using a red pencil, circle the article *the* every time it appears in our poem. What does the word *the* tell us is coming?

   b. Using a red pencil, underline the nouns, or naming words, that come after the article *the*.

   c. Using a blue pencil, underline the describing words, or adjectives, that come before several of the nouns.

   d. Read the sentences to your teacher, leaving out the adjectives. Now read them again, using the adjectives. Do the adjectives help you imagine the picture the author is describing?

   e. **SEE-SPELL-SAY:** Look and **see** each spelling word on the spelling list. **Spell** each word aloud. **Say** the word.

---

3. a. When we read a word, we can tell how many syllables it has by listening to how many sounds we hear. When you are counting the syllables in a word, clap each time you hear a part of the word. Words are usually divided between the consonant letters in words of more than one syllable.
   Ex: car/pet - 2 claps   hap/py - 2 claps
         hot - 1 clap   won/der/ful - 3 claps

Sidebar (left column):

✎ **Teacher's Note:**
As your student completes each lesson, choose skills from the *Review Activities* that he needs. The *Review Activities* follow each lesson.

✎ **Teacher's Note:**
If you choose to dictate, tell your student when to begin a new line. Also, tell him that in this poem, the first word in each line is capitalized.

See page 291.

2.
a. The article *the* tells us a noun is coming.

b. wind, winter, sun, fruits, garden

c. **Teacher's Note:**
Remind your student that sometimes an adjective, or describing word, is between the article and noun.

   cold, pleasant, summer, ripe

✎ **Teacher's Note:**
The word *summer* is usually a noun, but in this poem, *summer* is describing what kind of sun.

✎ **Teacher's Note:** The words *a*, *an*, and *the* are called articles and are also adjectives. It is acceptable if your student underlines these words.

See page 291.

b. When a word has two syllables, we usually divide the word between the middle two consonants. Sometimes, the middle two consonants are the same letter. We divide between the two consonant letters that are the same.

Draw a line between the two syllables of each of these words:

1) winter   3) summer   5) garden
2) purple   4) sunset   6) running

c. Here are some words with three syllables. Listen as your teacher reads them. Draw lines to show where to divide each syllable. Remember your rule about where to divide syllables.

1) afternoon   3) understood
2) tomorrow   4) yesterday

d. Read each word. Write 1, 2 or 3 on the line to show how many syllables are in each word.

1) ___ river   6) ___ morning
2) ___ sky   7) ___ wonderful
3) ___ beautiful   8) ___ small
4) ___ mountain   9) ___ headed
5) ___ great   10) ___ bright

e. Practice your spelling words with your Spelling Bee today.

a. Continue practicing the verse from this lesson using the method of choral reading you learned in Lesson 25, **4a**. Take turns reading each line and read the last line together.

b. Begin to memorize this verse, and continue to practice saying the other verses from memory as well.

c. Create a picture or two for this verse to go with the pictures you have for the other verses. Display your pictures while you are presenting the poem to your family.

d. You may want to give a practice presentation after you have learned the first three verses, or you can wait until you have learned the fourth verse and present the entire poem at one time.

✎ **Teacher's Note: The word *one* in the poem is used as a noun, and the word *every* is an adjective. The student is not expected to learn this at this time.**

3.
b. 1) win/ter
    2) pur/ple
    3) sum/mer
    4) sun/set
    5) gar/den
    6) run/ning

c. 1) af/ter/noon
    2) to/mor/row
    3) un/der/stood
    4) yes/ter/day

d. 1) 2
   2) 1
   3) 3
   4) 2
   5) 1
   6) 2
   7) 3
   8) 1
   9) 2
  10) 1

See page 291.

✏ **Teacher's Note:**
You will need index cards
or construction paper and
markers for this activity,
unless you use a
Sudent Activity Book.

e. Take your oral or written spelling pretest today.

★

5. a. Find the pages at the back of the *Student Activity Book*
labeled Lesson 26-5a-b and follow the directions in **5b**. Or,
use index cards, a colored marker, and two colors of
construction paper to make a deck of playing cards for this
game.

Write the word *noun* on the back of 20 cards. On the front of
each noun card, write one word from this list.

dog	car	box	boy	door
tree	book	coat	hat	flower
house	truck	sun	toy	girl
cat	table	bench	bed	ball

Write the word *adjective* on the back of 30 cards. On the
front of each adjective card, write one word from this list.

smart	pretty	fuzzy	hard	old
friendly	hot	round	soft	blue
loud	cold	red	tall	heavy
noisy	big	green	fast	wooden
torn	small	open	slow	fun
broken	happy	long	new	pink

b. How to Play: Mix the cards together, creating a deck of 50
cards. Deal out 7 cards to each player, placing the rest in a
stack face down. Each player's goal is to put down as many
noun-adjective matches as he can. After each match is laid
down, choose cards to replace the ones laid down. Each
player must keep seven cards in his hands until the final turn.
Then it is the next person's turn. Each noun-adjective pair
laid down must make sense. A noun can have up to two
adjectives to go with it, but no more than two adjectives per
noun. By the time all the cards are drawn, each person
counts the number of cards he has laid down (one point for
each) and subtracts one point for each card he is still
holding. The person with the most points wins.

c. Take your spelling test today.

wa

we

wu

wi

wh

wo

wt

wags

will

what

paws

went

won't

warm

1.
a. 3
b. 3
c. 3
d. 3

2. Possible answers.
a. beautiful
b. soft, strong, etc.
c. two, happy, etc.
d. red, broken, etc.

Review Activities

1. *Syllables*
   Write 1, 2, or 3 to show the number of syllables in each word. Draw lines to show where to divide each syllable.

   a. library
   b. dinosaur
   c. survival
   d. potato

2. *Adjectives*
   Fill in each blank with an adjective.

   a. We watched the _____ sunset.
   b. The _____ wind blew through the trees.
   c. John walked the _____ dogs.
   d. Where is the _____ crayon?

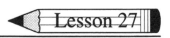

He gave us eyes to see them,
And lips that we might tell
How great is God Almighty,
Who has made all things well!

"The Creation" by Cecil Frances Alexander

a. Listen as your teacher reads the poem. Write the poem from dictation the second time she reads it, or copy it. Compare your copy to the literature passage and make corrections.

b. Copy the spelling words from *Focus on Spelling*. Say the words aloud as you write them. Some words spell the /e/ sound with **ea**.

> ### Focus on Spelling
> head   dead   bread   instead   ready
> **Bonus Word:** pleasant

 ★ ─────────────────────────────

a. We use some words to describe a verb or to tell us how something was done. These words are called **adverbs**. They answer the questions *how*, *when*, *where*, or *how much*. An adverb describes a verb, an adjective, or another adverb. In the last line of the verse, there is a word that tells us how God Almighty made all things. Underline this word.

> ### Grammar Guide
> **Adverb** - a word that describes
> a verb, an adjective, or another adverb

b. The word *well* in our literature passage tells us how God made all things. A word that is often used instead of the word *well* is the word *good*. They are not used the same way. *Good* describes people, places or things, but it can't tell how something was done. Here is a correct sentence:

That was a good dinner.

Good describes dinner. *Dinner* is a thing.

Teacher's Note:
As your student completes each lesson, choose skills from the *Review Activities* that he needs. The *Review Activities* follow each lesson.

Teacher's Note:
If you choose to dictate, tell your student when to begin a new line. Also, tell him that in this poem, the first word in each line is capitalized.

See page 291.

2.
a. well

b. no

Is this sentence correct?

He plays ball good.

Plays is not a thing. *Plays* is a doing word, so use *well*. *Well* tells how the playing was done.

Look at this sentence.

He plays ball well.

This sentence is correct. Listen to people use the words *well* and *good* in their conversations.

c. Read each sentence. Choose the word *good* or *well* to write in each blank.

1) We had a _____ time at the park.
2) This cookie is very _____.
3) The team played _____ today.
4) She painted that picture very_____.
5) My dad is a _____ fisherman.
6) Our fishing trip went _____.

d. **SEE-SPELL-SAY:** Look and **see** each word on the spelling list. **Spell** each word aloud. **Say** the word.

──────────────────────────────★

3. a. You have used many adjectives in the last four lessons. You are going to find synonyms, words that mean about the same thing, for each word. Here are words from our lessons.

1) beautiful   4) good
2) great   5) wonderful
3) wise   6) small

Look up each word in a thesaurus. The words in a thesaurus are in alphabetical order like a dictionary.

Write a brief list of synonyms for each word above. Tell your teacher a sentence using one of the synonyms you found for each word.

✎ **Teacher's Note:**
Good **is an adjective.**
Well **is an adverb.**

2.
c. 1) good
2) good
3) well
4) well
5) good
6) well

See page 291.

b. Read each of these sentences. Replace the italicized word
   with a synonym that you think fits best.

   1) Mother's new dress is *beautiful*.
   2) The king was a very *great* man.
   3) I don't think it is *wise* to play near the street.
   4) The sunny weather is *good*.
   5) Getting to see the mountains was *wonderful*.
   6) The new puppies are very *small*.

c. Practice your spelling words with a Spelling Bee today.

   ★ ───────────────────────────────

a. Listen as your teacher reads Genesis Chapter 1 to you.
   You will be asked to make a list of some of the things that
   Scripture says God created. God has been described in our
   verse as the one "Who has made all things well."
   That is a description of God as our Creator.

b. Use the *Student Activity Book* page provided, or fold a piece
   of paper into three parts as shown below. Label each section
   by writing at the top as shown.

Day 1	Day 2	Day 3

Now turn your paper over and continue labeling:

Day 4	Day 5	Day 6

3.
b. 1) lovely, pretty
   2) wonderful, grand
   3) smart, intelligent
   4) nice, pleasant
   5) terrific, marvelous
   6) tiny, little

See page 291.

4.

c. <u>Day 1</u>
  1. day
  2. night

<u>Day 2</u>
  1. heaven

<u>Day 3</u>
  1. earth
  2. seas
  3. plants
  4. trees

<u>Day 4</u>
  1. sun
  2. moon
  3. stars

<u>Day 5</u>
  1. creatures
    in the
    waters
  2. birds

<u>Day 6</u>
  1. living
    creatures
    on the
    earth
  2. man

d. He rested.

See page 291.

c. Make a list of several things that God made, as described in Genesis 1. Remember to number your list and to put a period after each number. Place each item on your list in the column of the day in which it was created.

d. After seeing all the things God made, you now know why He is called the Creator and why everything He made is called the Creation. Why didn't we have a Day 7 on our chart? What did God do on the seventh day of Creation?

e. Take your oral or written spelling pretest today.

5. a. Memorize the verse in this week's lesson, and continue to practice this and the other three verses in choral reading style as you learned in Lesson 25, **4a** (literature passages from Lessons 24-27).

b. Gather the pictures you have created for each verse. Put them in the correct order and practice your presentation, displaying your pictures.

c. Present all four verses of your poem. You can recite it (say it from memory) or present it as a choral reading, with other people taking part.

d. Optional: Take your spelling test today.

★

Handwriting
*Note: When connecting small **v** to other letters, the connecting line does not come down to the bottom line. The second letter starts from the middle of the line.

va

ve

vu

vi

vh

vo

vl

van

oven

invite

vest

over

wave

1.
a. well
b. well
c. well
d. good

2.
a. careful - cautious
b. breezy - windy
c. afraid - frightened
d. tired - weary
e. plain - simple

Review Activities

1. *Using* good *or* well

   Write the word *good* or *well* to complete these sentences.

   a. I played _____ at my baseball game.
   b. Have you been feeling _____?
   c. How _____ do you know Jim?
   d. The cake tastes _____.

2. *Synonyms*

   Match the words on the left to a synonym on the right.

   a. careful   weary
   b. breezy   frightened
   c. afraid   simple
   d. tired   cautious
   e. plain   windy

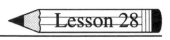

Teacher's Note:
As your student completes each lesson, choose skills from the *Review Activities* that he needs. The *Review Activities* follow each lesson.

Friendly Town Residential Listing

Brant, Ann	33 Daisy Drive	456 - 8632
Brent, Sally	40 Lily Lane	506 - 2488
Brown, Abe	212 Rose Road	321 - 0402
Brush, Bill	115 Tulip Trail	697 - 3565
Buster, Betty	65 Lily Lane	506 - 3992
Butternut, Bob	248 Tulip Trail	722 - 0191

Read the phone book listings silently as your teacher reads them aloud. Next, read them along with your teacher. Copy the listings, leaving a blank line between each name.

★

a. Look at the names listed. What is the same about all of them? What is different?

b. The names are listed in alphabetical order by last names. All the names listed start with **B**. Some of the names have the same first two letters. Using a red pencil, underline all the names that start with **Br**.

How do you think we put words in order that start with the same two letters?

c. With your red pencil, circle the third letter in each name beginning with **Br**. How are these names put in the correct order?

d. Look at the section of your real phone book with names starting with **Br**. Choose five names and write them on index cards. Mix them up and put them in the correct order.

Add the following entries to your phone book listings. Check with your teacher before you write them in to make sure you are putting them in the correct place:

Bride, Bonnie	10 Wedding Way	332 - 0113
Bumper, Bo	290 Pushy Place	799 - 8555

Teacher's Note:
A phone book with residential listings and index cards are needed for this lesson.

See page 292.

2.
a. All the names start with B.
   Some of them have the same first two letters; some do not.

b. Brant, Brent, Brown, Brush
   We use the third letter to know what order they go in.

c. Br**a**nt
   Br**e**nt
   Br**o**wn
   Br**u**sh
   They are in alphabetical order.

d. *Bonnie Bride goes between Brent and Brown. Bo Bumper goes between Brush and Buster.*

3.

a. 1) 65 Lily Lane
   2) 506 - 3992
   3) Sally Brent

b. 1) 115 Tulip Trail
   2) 697 - 3565
   3) Bob Butternut

c. ✏ **Teacher's Note:**
Teach this skill accordingly.
Students may use
grandparents, aunts,
uncles, etc.

3. a. As we saw in Lesson 5, we can learn much from a phone book. Look up the listing for Betty Buster. Tell your teacher these things about Betty:

   1) Where does Betty live?
   2) What is her phone number?
   3) Who else lives on the same street?

   b. Tell your teacher these things about Bill Brush.

   1) Where does Bill live?
   2) What is his phone number?
   3) Who else lives on the same street?

   c. Using your mother's or father's name, write the listing for your family as it would look in the phone book. Write the last name first and then your mother's or father's first name. Remember to begin names of people with a capital letter. Find your family's name, address, and phone number in your phone book. Compare what you wrote to the listing in the phone book.

   d. With your teacher's help, write down the names of three friends. Find them in the phone book. Either read the listing to your teacher or write them down. Now you have a start for your own address book.

4. a. Discuss with your teacher the correct way to use the telephone (such as how to answer the phone; or taking or leaving a message). With permission, call a friend. You may want to tell your friend what you have learned about the phone book.

   b. Review the spelling lists in Lessons 24-27.

See page 292.

★

. a. Either orally or in writing, spell the following words for your
teacher.

1) morning   We need to wake up early in the *morning*.
2) instead   I would like an apple *instead* of grapes.
3) bright   The light in the hall is very *bright*.
4) season   It is almost time for the summer *season*.
5) evening   I like to play outside in the *evening*.
6) ready   When will you be *ready* to go?
7) sunset   The *sunset* is beautiful this evening.
8) winter   We had a very cold *winter* this year.

b. Listen to your teacher as she dictates sentences to you.

1) The sunrise was bright on Sunday.
2) The fruit in the garden might be ready by summer.

c. After your teacher has checked your sentences, make any
corrections.

Cover your paper so that you can not see your corrected
sentence. Listen again to your teacher as she dictates the
same sentence again. Repeat the correction process.

5.

a.

✏ **Teacher's Note:**
**You may give sentences if
your student needs it to
understand the word given.**

b.

✏ **Teacher's Note:**
**Read the following
sentences to your student
to be written from dictation.
Read slowly, repeating
them several times.
Encourage your student to
just listen the first time, and
then begin. Do not be
concerned about saying it
too often. The goal is for
your student to be able to
write the sentence. Speed
and accuracy will be
increased over time.**

✏ **Teacher's Note:**
**After your student's first
attempt, show him how to
correct any mistakes. Read
the sentence again, several
times if needed. Repeat the
correction process.
Make sure to praise
improvements. He may
attempt it a third time if he
desires; however, be alert
to fatigue. If your student
is overly tired or
discouraged at this point, it
is best to end the session,
highlighting improvements.**

See page 292.

★

oats

boat

wait

vest

over

bowl

west

very

old

best

when

van

ox

brave

vote

word

only

wave

Review Activities

1. *Using a phone book*
   Look at this section of a telephone listing. Answer the following questions.

Keyser, Emily	720 Lantern Hill	813-3896
Klein, Todd	2142 Scenic Drive	214-1420
Koontz, Sharon	616 Edgewater Lane	367-2009
Kramer, William	1938 Scenic Drive	214-1709
Kress, Carol	1 426 King Avenue	439-8136
Kruger, Steven	815 Edgewater Lane	367-4700

a. What is Todd Klein's phone number?
b. What is Steven Kruger's address?
c. Who lives on the same road?

1.
a. 214-1420
b. 815 Edgewater Lane
c. Todd Klein and William Kramer live on Scenic Drive.

Sharon Koontz and Steven Kruger live on Edgewater Lane.

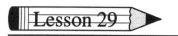

"Please, Etty, listen. I realize it must be difficult for you. But the point is, it's going to be a very bad flood. You have to leave the trolley. You can't stay here. You must move to higher ground," said Jeremy.

✎ Teacher's Note:
As your student completes each lesson, choose skills from the *Review Activities* that he needs. The *Review Activities* follow each lesson.

1. a. Listen as your teacher reads the literature passage. Write the literature passage from dictation the second time she reads it or copy it. Compare your copy to the literature passage and make corrections.

✎ Teacher's Note:
Remind your student that the literature passage contains a quotation.

   b. Copy the spelling words from *Focus on Spelling*. Say the words aloud as you write them. Some words spell the /oi/ sound with **oi**.

See page 292.

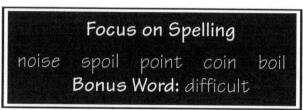

Focus on Spelling

noise   spoil   point   coin   boil
Bonus Word: difficult

2.
a. Jeremy

2. a. Read the literature passage silently to yourself. Who is speaking?

b. "Please, Etty, listen. I realize it must be difficult for you. But the point is, it's going to be a very bad flood. You have to leave the trolley. You can't stay here. You must move to higher ground."

   b. With a blue pencil, underline the words that Jeremy spoke.

   c. What punctuation mark shows you what Jeremy said?

c. Quotation marks enclose his words.

   d. Now, read the literature passage aloud to your teacher. Try to read the words Jeremy spoke as he would have spoken them.

e. six sentences

   e. How many sentences did Jeremy speak?

   f. How could you tell when a new sentence began?

f. A capital letter begins a sentence, and a period ends it.

   g. Although Jeremy spoke several sentences, they are all a part of what he said. A quotation mark is placed before his first spoken word and after his last spoken word.

h. This quotation ends with a comma. The comma is inside the closing quotation mark, followed by *said Jeremy*.

Please add quotation marks and commas in the following sentences. Remember to place the comma before the closing quotation mark.

1) Let's plant a garden said Rachel.
2) Yes, we can grow tomatoes said Jake.
3) I want to water the garden said Emily.

i. Complete the following quotation with something you might say.

"_____ ," said ___*(student's name)*___.

j. Try writing your own quotation.

k. **SEE-SPELL-SAY:** Look and **see** each spelling word on the spelling list. **Spell** each word aloud. **Say** the word.

a. A contraction is a shorter way of writing two words. An apostrophe (') replaces letter(s) that have been taken out. Find the two contractions in our literature passage and underline them.

b. Look at the words that go together to make up these contractions:

let us - let's   does not - doesn't

What letters were taken out?

c. Match the following words with their contractions:

can not	didn't
I am	it's
did not	can't
it is	I'll
I will	don't
do not	I'm

2.
h. 1) "Let's plant a garden," said Rachel.
   2) "Yes, we can grow tomatoes," said Jake.
   3) "I want to water the garden," said Emily.

i. Possible answer:
   "I want to read a book," said Sam.

3.
a. it's, can't

b. u in *let's*;
   o in *doesn't*

c. can not - can't
   I am   - I'm
   did not - didn't
   it is   - it's
   I will   - I'll
   do not - don't

3.
d. 1) I'm
   2) can't
   3) didn't
   4) I'll
   5) It's
   6) don't

4.
a. flood - an overflowing of water onto dry land

b. warn - to tell about danger

d. Use the contractions from **3c** in these sentence blanks:

1) (*I am*) going out to play.
2) Bob (*can not*) go fishing now.
3) We (*did not*) get to see the puppies.
4) (*I will*) get the bat and ball.
5) (*It is*) time to feed the puppies.
6) We (*do not*) have time to play ball.

e. Practice your spelling words in a Spelling Bee today.

4. a. From reading the literature passage, we can tell that there is going to be a flood. Look up the word *flood* in the dictionary. Discuss what a flood is with your teacher.

b. Jeremy has a job to do. He is supposed to warn the creatures on the riverbank about the coming flood. Look up the word *warn* or *warning* in the dictionary. Discuss its meaning with your teacher.

c. Has anyone ever warned you about something? Did you listen to the warning? What happened? Discuss this with your teacher.

d. Write a paragraph of three or four sentences about the warning you received. Using complete sentences, answer the following questions as a guideline. Remember to indent the first sentence in your paragraph. Begin each sentence with a capital letter and end it with a period.

1) What were you warned about?
2) Did you listen to the warning?
3) What did or did not happen?
4) How did you feel after it was over?

e. Take an oral or written spelling pretest today.

✏ **Teacher's Note:**
Remind your student of
any needed pronunciations
during reading.

5. a. Comprehension Check

Listen to your teacher as she reads the vocabulary words.
Read aloud the story, "Katie's Day at the Vet's Office."

Vocabulary

veterinary	vet	kennel	strange	monkeys	raccoons
squirrels	lizards	supplies	leashes	newspapers	
recycle	laundry	towels	groomer	finish	x-rays

Katie's Day at the Vet's Office
by Katie Bennett

One or two days a week, I help out at the veterinary office.
I ride my bike there, because it is so close to our house. I
really like working with animals. When I get there, I have a
list of things that I need to do. Before I start on my list, I
walk around the kennels and see what kinds of animals are
staying there. Usually there are just dogs, cats, and birds.
Sometimes there are strange animals like monkeys, raccoons,
squirrels, and lizards.

Now it is time to start my list. My first job is to refill
supplies. There are bags and leashes to put out and bottles to
refill. Next I am off to sort and stack newspapers. They
don't like to use the shiny ads in the cages. I take them out to
the recycle bin and stack the papers in a neat pile. Another
thing that I have to do is the laundry. Some of the cats and
dogs that stay there have blankets or towels in their kennels.

My favorite part is doing things with the animals. I have
to help clean the cages and walk the dogs. The cats all get
clean newspaper. Then I get to help the groomer. I wash a
dog while she trims and brushes a different dog or cat. We
wash the dogs in a regular bath tub that is up high so we don't
have to bend over.

That is about everything on my list that I have to do.
When I finish my list, I walk around to see if anyone needs
any help. Sometimes I get to help the veterinarian. Usually
he has me hold the animals while he looks at it. Other times,
I take the lunch order, file papers and x-rays, or clean up
something.

After we eat lunch or I get tired of working, I ride my bike home. I always have a fun time working at the vet.

(Katie Bennett is a fourteen year old homeschooler who lives in Indialantic, Florida.)

b. Discuss the following questions with your teacher.

Discussion Questions

1) What does a veterinarian, or vet, do? Why does Katie help out at the vet's office?
2) What kinds of animals are usually at the vet's office? What different kinds of animals are there sometimes?
3) What are some of the jobs Katie has to do before she works with the animals?
4) Why does Katie wash blankets and towels at the vet's office?
5) What does Katie get to do with the dogs? What does she do with the cats?
6) How does Katie get to help the vet?
7) Does Katie like working at the vet's office? Would you like to help at the vet's office?
8) What things do you think Katie is learning by helping at the vet's office?

c. Optional: Take your spelling test today.

★

5.
b. 1) A veterinarian is a doctor that takes care of animals. She helps because she likes working with animals.
2) Dogs, cats, and birds are usually at the vet's office. Sometimes there are monkeys, raccoons, squirrels, or lizards.
3) She has to refill supplies and sort and stack newspapers.
4) Katie washes blankets and towels because the animals have them in their kennels, and they get dirty.
5) Katie walks the dogs and cleans the cats' cages. She helps the groomer wash the dogs.
6) Sometimes she helps the vet by holding an animal while he looks at it.
7) Katie always has fun working at the vet's office.
8) Answers will vary.

See page 292.

As

An

All

Am

Come

Call

Cub

City

Only

Oats

Olive

Over

Quick

Queen

Quit

Question

1. Joan asked, "May I have a cookie?"

2.
a. I will
b. do not
c. can not
d. it is or it has

3. a capital letter

4. indent

Review Activities

1. *Quotation Marks.*
   Add quotation marks.

   Joan asked, May I have a cookie?

2. *Contractions*
   What words do these contractions replace?

   a. I'll
   b. don't
   c. can't
   d. it's

3. *Capitalization*
   How do you begin every sentence?

4. *Paragraph*
   How do you begin every paragraph?

Assessment 6
(Lessons 24 - 29)

1. Add adjectives, or describing words, to these sentences.

   a. Sam rode his _____ bike.
   b. He beeped his _____ horn.
   c. It made a _____ noise.
   d. Sam is a _____ boy.

2. Add the suffix **-ful** to these words.

   a. play
   b. care
   c. thought
   d. rest

3. Circle the articles and underline the nouns.

   a. A child fell into the water.
   b. The boy laughed at the clown.
   c. A lion roared at the crowd.

4. Underline the nouns and draw an arrow from the adjective to the noun it describes.

   The tall man was walking his gray dog.

5. Write the contractions.

   a. I will
   b. can not
   c. it is
   d. do not

---

1. **Possible answers.**
a. **new, shiny**
b. **bike, red**
c. **loud, squeaky**
d. **nice, happy**

2.
a. **playful**
b. **careful**
c. **thoughtful**
d. **restful**

3.
a. Ⓐ **child** fell into **the** **water**.
b. **The** **boy** laughed at the **clown**.
c. Ⓐ **lion** roared at **the** **crowd**.

4. **The tall man was walking his gray dog.**

5.
a. **I'll**
b. **can't**
c. **it's**
d. **don't**

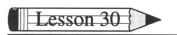

✎ **Teacher's Note:**
As your student completes each lesson, choose skills from the *Review Activities* that he needs. The *Review Activities* follow each lesson.

The little black moorhen strutted here and there, poking into this and that. In the end, she turned to Jeremy and said, "Oh, I don't know. Let the flood take it all. I'll make a new nest when I come back."

The Tale of Jeremy Vole, Copyright 1990 by Stephen Lawhead. Published by Lion Publishing Corporation. All rights reserved. Used by permission.

✎ **Teacher's Note:**
Remind your student that the literature passage contains a quotation.

1. a. Listen as your teacher reads the literature passage. Write the poem from dictation the second time she reads it, or copy it. Compare your copy to the literature passage and make corrections.

   b. Copy the spelling words from *Focus on Spelling*. Say the words aloud as you write them. Words may spell the /oo/ sound with **oo**, **ew**, and **ue**.

> ### Focus on Spelling
> new   glue   tool   soup   flew
> **Bonus Word:** juice

See page 292.

2.

a. don't, I'll

b. "Oh, I don't know.
Let the flood take it all.
I'll make a new nest
when I come back."

2. a. In Lesson 29, you reviewed how to write contractions. You will continue that review, as well as add some new contractions to your list. Underline the contractions in our literature passage.

   b. Remember that you use an apostrophe (') to take the place of letter(s) that you leave out when you join two words. Cross out the letters you leave out to make these contractions.

Ex: she is - she i̶s̶

b.

1) I a̶m	6) you a̶re
2) we a̶re	7) was no̶t
3) is no̶t	8) we wi̶ll
4) does no̶t	9) I h̶ave
5) do no̶t	10) are no̶t

1) I am	6) you are
2) we are	7) was not
3) is not	8) we will
4) does not	9) I have
5) do not	10) are not

c. Write the correct contraction in each blank.
   1) (*I have*) _____ washed my shirt.
   2) We (*are not*) _____ going to the store.
   3) Mother will make a snack when (*we are*) _____ done.
   4) She (*is not*) _____ on my soccer team.
   5) The dog (*does not*) _____ wear its collar.
   6) Dad said (*you are*) _____ going to the game.
   7) Bob said (*we will*) _____ be in the play.
   8) This (*was not*) _____ the book I wanted to read.

d. Read the literature passage silently. The little, black moorhen is speaking to Jeremy. Read the exact words the moorhen said, just as she would have spoken them.

e. How did you know which words were the moorhen's words?

f. **SEE-SPELL-SAY:** Look and **see** each spelling word on the spelling list. **Spell** each word aloud. **Say** the word.

a. The literature passage tells about some new kinds of animals. Look up the word *vole* in the encyclopedia, using the volume marked V. (You may also use an encyclopedia on the computer.) Answer the following questions.

   1) Where do these animals usually live?
   2) What do they look like?

   You may add any other information.

b. Do the same thing looking up *moorhen* in the encyclopedia. Use the volume marked M.

c. Use the chart in your *Student Activity Book* or fold a piece of paper down the middle vertically, like this:

vole	moorhen

2.
c. 1) I've
   2) aren't
   3) we're
   4) isn't
   5) doesn't
   6) you're
   7) we'll
   8) wasn't

e. Quotation marks enclose the exact words spoken.

3.
a. Suggested answers:
   1) They live in fields and meadows near water.
   2) They look like mice.

b. Suggested answers:
   1) They live in marshes or on the side of a lake.
   2) waterbird about 13 in. long, with a short red bill

At the top of one side, write the word *vole*. At the top of the other side, write the word *moorhen*. List the facts you know about each animal under each heading. You do not need to write complete sentences.

d. Look at your lists of facts and find at least one fact that is the same about each creature. Now look at the lists and find at least one fact that is different. These similarities and differences are called **compare** and **contract**. Point these o to your teacher.

e. Practice your spelling words with your Spelling Bee today.

4.
a. litt<u>le</u>

4. a. The letters **le** at the end of a word usually says /l/.

   Ex: apple   candle

   Find the word in our literature passage that has the **-le** say /l Write the word and underline **-le**.

b. shov<u>el</u>, trav<u>el</u>

b. The letters **el** at the end of a word can also say /l/. There are fewer words using this spelling.

   Write these words and underline the two letters that make th /l/ sound: shovel   travel

c. The letters **al** at the end of the word can also say /l/.

   Write these words and underline the two letters that make th /l/ sound: petal   final

c. pet<u>al</u>, fin<u>al</u>

Phonics Fact
The letters **-le**, **-el**, and **-al** at the end of a word say /l/.

d. Use the *Student Activity Book* page provided, or fold a piece of paper into thirds, like this:

- le	- el	- al

At the top of each column, write these headings: **le, el, al**. Then write each word in the category that shows the correct /l/ sound.

middle	metal	bottle	circle	handle
nickel	castle	animal	oval	final
battle	squirrel	uncle	travel	petal
people	shovel	table	settle	several

e. Optional: Take your spelling pretest today.

5. a. Read the literature passage aloud to your teacher. How does the moorhen seem to be acting? What do you think she is feeling?

b. In the literature passage, a picture has been painted of Etty's feelings with words. Try to find the two phrases in the first sentence that show you that Etty is worried and upset.

c. The phrases, "here and there" and "this and that," give us a feeling of Etty going back and forth, trying to make a decision. Read this sentence for your teacher:

When we went into the store, Mom looked at this and that.

What did Mom look at in the store? Do we know from this sentence exactly what she looked at?

---

d. <u>le</u>   **<u>al</u>**
uncle   **metal**
people   **oval**
handle   **animal**
settle   **several**
circle   **petal**
middle   **final**
bottle
castle   **<u>el</u>**
table   **nickel**
battle   **squirrel**
               travel
               shovel

See page 292.

5.
a. Etty seems to be very upset and nervous.

b. strutted here and there poking into this and that

c. Mom looked at this and that.
No, we don't know what she looked at.

See page 292. ───────

d. These expressions, "here and there" and "this and that" show that a decision has not yet been made. The sentence in **5c** shows that Mom hadn't really looked at anything specifically. Make up at least one sentence using each expression.

e. Optional: Take your spelling test today.

★

Hi

Hello

Hat

Hot

Hurry

Mom

Make

Most

Meal

Mix

Nate

Near

No

Night

Nurse

Review Activities

1. *Contractions*
   Write the correct contraction in each blank.

   a. I hope (*you are*) _____ coming.

   b. (*We are*) _____ going on vacation.

   c. I (*have not*) _____ seen my grandma in a long time.

   d. She (*does not*) _____ know that we are coming.

2. *Spelling*
   Circle the word that is spelled incorrectly in each group.

   a. castle   middle   people   shovle

   b. travel   squirrel   tabel   nickel

   c. final   battal   animal   oval

1.
a. you're
b. We're
c. haven't
d. doesn't

2.
a. shovle (shovel)
b. tabel (table)
c. battal (battle)

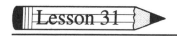

The moorhen's thanks gave Jeremy a warm feeling as he continued on his way. "Finally," he thought to himself, "someone finally listened to me. Someone believed."

The Tale of Jeremy Vole, Copyright 1990 by Stephen Lawhead. Published by Lion Publishing Corporation. All rights reserved. Used by permission.

Teacher's Note:
This literature passage contains a split quotation. This skill will be more thoroughly taught in a higher level book.

1. a. Listen as your teacher reads the literature passage. Write th poem from dictation the second time she reads it, or copy it. Watch the quotation marks and commas. Compare your cop to the literature passage and make corrections.

   b. Copy the spelling words from *Focus on Spelling*. Say the words aloud as you write them. Some words spell the /ē/ sound with **ie**.

See page 292.

Focus on Spelling

chief   believe   field   piece   yield
Bonus Word: finally

★

2. a. In our literature passage, Jeremy is thinking some thoughts that have been shared with you, the reader. Quotation marks (" ") are used to show us someone is speaking and what is said. In this case, the quotation marks are also used to show Jeremy's thoughts. Circle the quotation marks.

2.
b. "Finally, someone finally listened to me. Someone believed."

   b. Not all of the literature passage is part of Jeremy's thoughts, only the words that are inside the quotation marks. Quotatic marks are placed around the actual words spoken or thought Underline <u>only</u> Jeremy's thoughts.

   c. Ask your teacher this question:

   "What will we do after this lesson?"

   Now, write down her answer. Place a comma after her last word. Place quotation marks around all the words which were spoken. Be sure to place the closing quotation mark after the comma. Next to the closing quotation mark, write *said the teacher.* Place a period at the end of the sentence.

230

Ex: "We will have a snack," said the teacher.

Now ask your teacher to read this question to you:

"What is your favorite snack?"

Write down your answer using quotation marks.

Ex: "My favorite snack is raisins," said _(student's name)_ .

d. **SEE-SPELL-SAY:** Look and **see** each spelling word on the spelling list. **Spell** each word aloud. **Say** the word.

★ ——————————————————— **See page 293.**

a. The suffix **-ed** has been added to several words in our literature passage to show that something has already happened. Make a list of the three words from the literature passage that end with **-ed**.

b. Draw a line between the suffix **-ed** and the base word on all three words.

Ex: lik/ed   jump/ed

c. Are all the base words spelled correctly without the suffix?

When the suffix **-ed** is added to a base word ending with a silent **e**, you drop the **e** before adding the suffix.

d. Add **-ed** to each of these words.

1) love   5) bake
2) show   6) pass
3) talk   7) play
4) please   8) name

e. Let's review how you show that something has already happened (past tense).

1) Most words just add the suffix **-ed**.
2) Short words ending in a short vowel and a consonant double the last consonant before adding **-ed**.
3) Words ending in a silent **e** drop the **e** before adding **-ed**.

3.
a. continued, listened, believed

b. continu/ed, listen/ed, believ/ed

c. No, an *e* needs to be added to the end of the words *continue* and *believe*.

d.
1) loved   baked
2) showed   passed
3) talked   played
4) pleased   named

4) Words ending in a consonant and **y**, change the **y** to **i** before adding **-ed**.
5) Words ending in a vowel and **y**, just add **-ed**.
6) Some words (irregular words) change their spelling completely.

Write a word to fill each blank.

1) Today, I *walk*. Yesterday, I _____.
2) Today, I *hop*. Yesterday, I _____.
3) Today, I *like*. Yesterday, I _____.
4) Today, I *hurry*. Yesterday, I _____.
5) Today, I *pray*. Yesterday, I _____.
6) Today, I *tell*. Yestereday, I _____.

f. Practice your spelling words with your Spelling Bee today.

e. 1) walked
** 2) hopped**
** 3) liked**
** 4) hurried**
** 5) prayed**
** 6) told**

4. a. The sound /**er**/ is spelled several ways. The most common way this sound is spelled is **er**, **ir**, and **ur**.

4.
a. driv<u>er</u>   lat<u>er</u>
**   s<u>ir</u>   th<u>ir</u>d**
**   b<u>ur</u>n   n<u>ur</u>se**

driver	later
sir	third
burn	nurse

Underline the two letters in each of these words that spell the /**er**/ sound.

b. The /**er**/ sound at the end of a word is sometimes spelled **ar**.

b. doll<u>ar</u>   cell<u>ar</u>
c. col<u>or</u>   doct<u>or</u>

dollar   cellar

Underline the two letters in each word that spell the /**er**/ sound.

c. A third way to spell the /**er**/ sound is with **or** at the end of a word.

color   doctor

Underline the two letters in each word that spell the /**er**/ sound.

d. Use the page provided in your *Student Activity Book* or fold a piece of paper into thirds, like this:

-er	-ar	-or

At the top of each column, write these headings: **er**, **ar**, **or**. Then write each word in the category that shows how the /er/ sound is spelled.

pitcher	motor	sugar	river
dollar	together	remember	cellar
mirror	hammer	wonder	collar
color	another	doctor	summer

e. Take your oral or written spelling pretest today.

★

a. Something special has happened for Jeremy. Discuss this with your teacher.

b. Pretend you are Jeremy, and tell your teacher what has happened with Etty and why it has been so encouraging. Tell her what it is you (Jeremy) have been trying to do.

c. In the Bible, a young man named David also had a problem with people believing him. Retell the story of David and Goliath to your teacher, or listen as she reads it to you from I Samuel 17:28 - 51.

d. Together with your teacher or other students, act out the story of David and Goliath. Why do you think Eliab, his brother, and King Saul didn't think David could kill Goliath? Compare the similarities between the story of David and Goliath and the story of Jeremy and the Riverbank creatures.

e. Optional: Take your spelling test today.

4.
d. **er**
hammer	pitcher
wonder	river
remember	summer
together	another

ar
sugar	collar
cellar	dollar

or
motor	mirror
doctor	color

See page 293.

5.
a. **Someone finally believed Jeremy. It gave him a warm feeling.**

d. **Eliab and Saul didn't think David could kill Goliath because he was so young, and not strong and impressive looking.**

The stories are similar because others had trouble believing in David and Jeremy because they did not appear big and strong. They didn't know whether or not what David and Jeremy were saying was true. They underestimated those who were trying to help.

When

Water

Went

Woke

What

Very

Vase

Visit

Vest

Van

Us

Under

Use

Upon

Uncle

Review Activities

Choose the skills your student needs to review.

1. *Quotation marks*
   Underline the actual words spoken or thought.

   a. "I wonder if Tom is home," thought Robert.
   b. "I will ask Jason," he thought to himself.
   c. "Let's go see if Tom is home," said Jason.
   d. "Good idea!" replied Robert.

2. *Suffix -ed*
   Add the suffix **-ed** to these words.

   a. wash
   b. rally
   c. marry
   d. pat
   e. poke

1.
a. "I wonder if Tom is home," thought Robert.
b. "I will ask Jason," he thought to himself.
c. "Let's go see if Tom is home," said Jason.
d. "Good idea!" replied Robert.

2.
a. washed
b. rallied
c. married
d. patted
e. poked

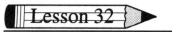

Teacher's Note:
As your student completes each lesson, choose skills from the *Review Activities* that he needs. The *Review Activities* follow each lesson.

Teacher's Note:
If your student does not have a *Student Activity Book*, you will need index cards to prepare an antonym matching game on Day 5.

See page 293.

2

a. easier, harder, stronger, deeper, faster

b. easi/er, hard/er, strong/er, deep/er, fast/er
The word *easier* changed its spelling,

c. When a word ends with a consonant and *y*, change the *y* to an *i* and add -*er*. When a word ends with a consonant, just add -*er*.

That one small victory made it easier to carry on. He paddled all the harder. The current was stronger now, the water deeper and moving faster.

The Tale of Jeremy Vole, Copyright 1990 by Stephen Lawhead. Published by Lion Publishing Corporation. All rights reserved. Used by permission.

1. a. Listen as your teacher reads the literature passage. Write these sentences from dictation the second time she reads them, or copy them. Compare your copy to the literature passage and make corrections.

   b. Copy the spelling words from *Focus on Spelling*. Say the words aloud as you write them. Some words spell the /**er**/ sound with **ur** and **ear**.

   > ## Focus on Spelling
   > current   turn   early   learn   hurry
   > **Bonus Word:** victory

2. a. In Lesson 31, we looked at words that had the suffix **-ed** added to them. In this lesson, underline the words with the suffix **-er** added. The suffix **-er** often means more of something when used at the end of an adjective.

   b. Write down the adjectives you underlined, and draw a line between **-er** and the base word. Look at the base, or root word, and see if you think it is spelled correctly.

   c. All the base words stayed the same, except for *easier*. The base word is *easy*. Tell your teacher how the word *easy* was changed to add the suffix **-er**.

Write new words by adding the suffix **-er** to each of these base words:

1) dirty   5) sick
2) dark   6) hungry
3) dry   7) quick
4) small   8) heavy

d. Fill in these sentences with one of the words you made in **2c**.

1) By dinner time, she was _____than Mom.
2) The rabbit is _____than the turtle.
3) The night seems _____without the moon's light.
4) My piece of cake is _____than yours.
5) Bob feels so sick. He is _____than Ted.
6) The sand is much _____before it rains.
7) The boy is dirty, but the baby is _____.
8) The couch is _____than the chair.

e. **SEE-SPELL-SAY:** Look and **see** each spelling word on the spelling list. **Spell** each word aloud. **Say** the word.

a. We have now read four literature passages from our story about Jeremy Vole. Do you think this is a true or make-believe story? Why do you think so?

b. Stories that are real or true are called nonfiction, while stories that are make-believe are called fiction. Is our story fiction or nonfiction?

c. The words fiction and nonfiction are important because they help us know where to look for certain kinds of books in the library. Gather together at least five books in your home (or library) that are nonfiction, or true stories. Make another collection of five fiction (or make-believe) books.

d. You are going to make two lists, like this:

Nonfiction Books	Fiction Books
1.	1.
2.	2.
3.	3.
4.	4.
5.	5.

2.
1) dirtier
2) darker
3) drier
4) smaller
5) sicker
6) hungrier
7) quicker
8) heavier

d. 1) hungrier
2) quicker
3) darker
4) smaller
5) sicker
6) drier
7) dirtier
8) heavier

3.
a. **This is a make-believe story because animals can't talk.**

b. **fiction**

Write the names of your books into these spaces. Make sure you start the first word in each of the titles with a capital letter. Capitalize every other important word and underline the entire title.

Ex: <u>The Tale of Jeremy Vole</u>

e. Practice your spelling words today.

★

See page 293.

4.

a. The victory was that the moorhen believed Jeremy's warning. After telling many creatures about the coming flood, this was the first sign that Jeremy's work was doing some good.

b. The current was stronger now, the water deeper and moving faster.

4. a. Discuss with your teacher the meaning of the word *victory*. Why do you think this is a victory for Jeremy?

b. Do you think all of Jeremy's struggles are over? Read the sentence to your teacher that tells how things are going for Jeremy.

c. When you are having a hard time with something, would it help you to have a "small victory?" Do you think Jeremy will give up now?

d. Draw a picture (or pictures) of Jeremy and his struggles.

e. Take your spelling pretest today.

★

See page 293.

✎ **Teacher's Note:**
Use the page in the back of the *Student Activity Book* labeled Lesson 32-5a, or write these words on index cards or construction paper squares. Put the number on the corner of the front, so that the student can make sure his matches are correct.

5. a. Your teacher will give you a set of cards with antonyms (or words that are opposites) on them. Each antonym ends with the suffix **-er**. Turn the cards face down. Take turns with a partner trying to make a match by turning over two cards at a time. If they are opposites, it is a match. Keep the cards and take another turn. The player with the most cards wins, but you may play several times so everyone gets a chance to win.

b. Optional: Take your spelling test today.

1.	taller	1.	shorter
2.	faster	2.	slower
3.	harder	3.	softer
4.	drier	4.	wetter
5.	cleaner	5.	dirtier
6.	darker	6.	lighter
7.	sooner	7.	later
8.	louder	8.	quieter
9.	bigger	9.	smaller
10.	happier	10.	sadder

X-ray

Xerox

Xenon

Xylophone

Yard

Yellow

You

Yummy

Yip

Zipper

Zero

Zoo

Review Activities

1. *Suffix -er*
   Add the suffix **-er** to these words.

   a. tall
   b. messy
   c. kind
   d. slow
   e. happy

2. Write *fiction* or *nonfiction* to make these sentences true.

   a. A story that tells about something true is called
      _____.

   b. A story that tells about something that is make-
      believe is called _____.

1.
a. taller
b. messier
c. kinder
d. slower
c. happier

2.
a. nonfiction
b. fiction

1. "I would like to go to the
   park," thought Justin.
b. "Let's go to the park
   to play," said Mom.
c. "Hurray! Let's go!"
   said Willy.
d. "I'll pack a lunch,"
   said Katy.

2.
a. waited
b. buried
c. shopped
d. raked

3.
a. smaller
b. sillier
c. colder
d. funnier

Assessment 7
(Lessons 30 - 32)

1. Underline the actual words spoken or thought.

   a. "I would like to go to the park," thought Justin.
   b. "Let's go to the park to play," said Mom.
   c. "Hurray! Let's go!" said Willy.
   d. "I'll pack a lunch," said Katy.

2. Add the suffix **-ed** to these words.

   a. wait   _____
   b. bury   _____
   c. shop   _____
   d. rake   _____

3. Add the suffix **-er** to these words.

   a. small   _____
   b. silly   _____
   c. cold   _____
   d. funny   _____

a. In this lesson, you are going to solve mysteries that use words and letters. That would make you a detective. Tell your teacher what a detective is. (If you don't know what a detective is, look up this word in the dictionary, and explain its meaning to your teacher.)

The story you are going to read in this lesson is about a boy named Encyclopedia Brown. He is ten-years-old and lives in a town called Idaville. Encyclopedia (his real name is Leroy) loves to help his father solve cases. His father is the Chief of Police in Idaville.

Have you heard or read about any other famous detectives? Tell your teacher what you think would make someone a good detective.

b. Find the story "Encyclopedia Brown and the Case of the Forgetful Sheriff." Look over the story and point out any new or unknown words to your teacher. Make a list of these words, and your teacher will explain the meaning of each word. Read the story orally or silently.

Teacher's Note:
Explain to your student any unfamiliar words he lists. Allow your student to choose the method of reading that he is most comfortable with. If the story seems too difficult, you may read it to your student and have him read it to you at another time.

Encyclopedia Brown and the Case of the Forgetful Sheriff

Led by Mr. Scotty, the party of eastern tourists rode the Texas range. The hotel manager had promised them "Historic Scenes of the Old Wild West." Who knew what another mile might bring?

Encyclopedia Brown knew. More blisters.

He rode last in line. Behind him came only the chuck wagon with the food. Around noon, even the chuck wagon passed him.

Encyclopedia didn't mind. It was lunch time.

Most of the tourists (including Encyclopedia) ate standing up. It made the boy detective mad to see his father sitting contentedly on the ground.

"You don't look well, Leroy," he said.

"I wish Bugs Meany were sitting in my place," said Encyclopedia.

Chief Brown grinned. "I had the cowboy at the hotel give you the gentlest horse in the stable."

"Then I must have the toughest saddle," answered Encyclopedia. "Say, Dad, do you think I made Mr. Scotty mad before?"

"No, but you upset him when you figured out the truth about the gunfight between Ringo Charlie and Johnny Kid," replied his father.

"I'll try to keep still," vowed Encyclopedia.

For the next half hour of riding there was little else to do. The horses plodded across flat grasslands. At last Mr. Scotty called, "Dismount here, folks."

The skinny little guide led the way to a pocket formed by nine high rocks.

"Now this here spot is called Outlaw Cemetery. It was so named on account of the five outlaws done in here eighty years ago," he began.

"Them outlaws held up the bank at River Falls. They escaped with twelve thousand dollars in gold," said Mr. Scotty.

"Sheriff Wiggins immediately set out after the desperadoes. But he was new on the job and forgetful. He forgot to put on his six-gun."

Mr. Scotty paused. He looked at the crowd of tourists to see if everyone was paying attention. He looked especially at Encyclopedia.

Then he resumed his tale.

"One of the citizens of River Falls happened to enter the sheriff's office. He saw the sheriff's six-gun still on the desk. Quickly he spread the word. A posse of citizens was rounded up to ride out and help the unarmed lawman capture the bank robbers. About ten miles out of town the posse heard gun play. When the shooting stopped, the posse rode up to this here spot. Stretched out dead as fish in a barrel were them five outlaws."

Mr. Scotty began hopping about as he warmed to his tale.

"Sheriff Wiggins," he said, "had recovered the stolen gold. But he was wounded in his left arm. In his modest way, he told the posse what had happened. He said the lookout for the outlaws saw him coming and shot two bullets into his left arm."

Suddenly Mr. Scotty clutched his left arm above the elbow. Then he made a leap and began to throw himself around.

"Sheriff Wiggins said he wrestled the lookout's pearl-handled six-gun away despite his wounded left arm. Then he shot the lookout with his own gun—a bullet through the heart it was."

At this point, Mr. Scotty dropped to one knee. "Right away the other four outlaws came at Sheriff Wiggins shooting up a storm," he said. "But the sheriff was cool as a hog on ice. He drilled them four desperadoes—*bang*! *bang*! *bang*! *bang*! in four seconds flat."

The skinny little guide jumped to his feet. He was breathing heavily with the effort of acting out the heroic sheriff's one-man stand against the five outlaws.

"The outlaws were buried on boothill," he continued. "The stolen gold was returned to the bank at River Falls. Everybody in town claimed Sheriff Wiggins ought to run for president."

Mr. Scotty dusted himself off carefully, letting the tourists wait for more of the story.

Then he said, "The town gave a dinner for the sheriff, though he said he didn't deserve the honor. Why, he was only doing his duty getting back the stolen gold, he said. But Mr. Baker, the bank president, disagreed."

Again Mr. Scotty broke off his tale to look at the tourists. He shot Encyclopedia a sly glance. It seemed to say, "Ready to solve this one, sonny?"

"Mr. Baker," concluded Mr. Scotty, "said Sheriff Wiggins had done a mite more than his duty. And since this was the lawman's last meal, he'd better eat well. Then Mr. Baker said something that made the three biggest men at the dinner seize Sheriff Wiggins. Somebody got a rope, and at sunrise they hanged the lawman!"

The tourists gasped in amazement.

After a brief silence, a lady from Vermont asked, "What did Mr. Baker say that made them hang the sheriff?"

"Why, now, that's the puzzle, isn't it?" replied Mr. Scotty, "I don't expect that anybody here could solve it, could he?"

The skinny little guide did not mention anyone by name. But the grown-ups on the tour turned and looked at Encyclopedia.

Chief Brown looked at him, too.

"Should I speak out, Dad?" asked Encyclopedia.

"If you know what Mr. Baker said that made the citizens

hang Sheriff Wiggins," said his father.

Encyclopedia took a step forward. "Mr. Baker said that—"

WHAT DID MR. BAKER SAY?

Mr. Baker said:

"You can't shoot seven bullets from a six-gun."

Count them.

Sheriff Wiggins claimed: he was wounded in the left arm by two shots (two bullets) from the lookout's six-gun; he then seized the lookout's gun and killed him with it (three bullets) then he shot the remaining four outlaws (seven bullets!).

Encyclopedia reasoned (as had Mr. Baker) that the sheriff was secretly a member of the holdup gang. In riding after his outlaw partners, the lawman didn't bother to put on his gun because he didn't think he'd need it.

Then he had a falling out over the division of the loot, probably. Getting hold of a gun, he surprised and killed his partners.

Before he could ride off with the gold, the posse reached him. So he had to make up the story about shooting the five outlaws in the line of duty.

From *Encyclopedia Brown* and *The Case of the Secret Pitch* by Donald Sobol. Copyright © 1965 Donald J. Sobol. Used by permission of Dutton Children's Books, a division of Penguin Books USA Inc.

1.

c. 1) Texas

2) Outlaw Cemetery

3) Outlaws had stolen twelve thousand dollars worth of gold from a bank. Sheriff Wiggins chased after them.

4) His six-gun

5) They were all shot and killed.

6) The sheriff said that he had surprised and killed all five of the outlaws.

7) The banker pointed out that the sheriff had claimed to have fired seven bullets from a six-gun.

c. Discuss the following questions with your teacher after you have read the story.

1) In what state does this story take place?
2) To what special place did the guide take the group?
3) What had outlaws stolen 80 years before? Who had chased after them?
4) What did Sheriff Wiggins forget?
5) What happened to the outlaws?
6) What did Sheriff Wiggins say happened?
7) What did Mr. Baker, the bank president, say?

d. With your teacher, review the list of the new or unknown
   words you made. Try to read them for your teacher. If there
   are any words you do not know the meaning of, look them up
   in the dictionary or discuss them with your teacher.

a. You have done several wordsearch puzzles in this book.
   Complete these simple wordsearches to prepare you for the
   larger wordsearch puzzle in **2d**. Find the word *cat*, and circle
   it:

```
R   C   B
L   A   M
E   T   S
```

b. This word was written from top to bottom. Some words are
   hidden from left to right (or side to side). Find the word *dog*,
   and circle it:

```
B   N   E
L   P   S
D   O   G
```

c. When you do a wordsearch, often letters are shared by more
   than one word, like in a crossword puzzle. Here is an
   example. Find the words *big* and *bat*, and circle each word
   separately:

```
B   I   G
A   O   Z
T   L   Y
```

d. Now you are ready to find the following words in the
   wordsearch puzzle. A good way to search for a word is to
   look at the first two letters of the word, then check each row
   going across for those two letters next to each other. Start at
   the top row, and check each row in order. If you don't find
   them, check each row going from top to bottom for the two
   letters next to each other. Again, start on the left side and
   check each row, moving over one row each time until you
   find the word. Here are your words to find. (Notice all the
   words and letters are capital letters.)

2.

a.

b.

c.

Brown	Sheriff	Texas
Leroy	Gold	Horse
Sixgun	Bank	

2.

d.

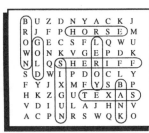

```
B U Z D N Y A C K J
R J F P H O R S E M
O G E C S F L Q W U
W O N K V G E P D K
N L Q S H E R I F F
S D W I P D O C L Y
F Y J X M F Y S B P
H K Z G U T E X A S
V D I U L A J H N V
A C P N R S W Q K O
```

If you want to do more wordsearches, there are many bookstores and grocery stores that sell them.

3.

a. BEACH

3. a. Another kind of word puzzle is called a letter number puzzle. Each letter in the alphabet is assigned a number. When you see each number, you are to find the letter it represents in the key and write it on the line. After you write all the letters, you should be able to read a word. Another word for this kind of puzzle is a code. Try this puzzle:

KEY							
A	B	C	D	E	F	G	H
7	3	1	2	5	8	6	9

   __   __   __   __   __

   3   5   7   1   9

b. You should have made the word *beach* in our last section. As you can see, the numbers are not in order. Sometimes, the letters in the key box may not be in alphabetical order either. Try to solve this puzzle:

KEY												
A	E	I	O	U	B	C	D	F	G	H	J	K
5	10	15	20	25	1	2	3	4	6	7	8	9

__ __ __ __   __ __ __ __
5   1 15 6   2   5 9 10

c. Here is a coded message for you to figure out:

KEY												
B	C	D	F	G	H	J	K	L	M	N		
6	7	8	9	10	11	12	13	14	15	16		
P	Q	R	S	T	V	W	X	Y	Z			
17	18	19	20	21	22	23	24	25	26			
A	E	I	O	U								
1	2	3	4	5								

__   __ __ __ __   __ __
3   14 3 13 2   21 4

__ __ __ __   __ __ __ __ __
19 2 1 8   1 6 4 5 21

__ __ __ __ __ __ __ __ __ __.
8 2 21 2 7 21 3 22 2 20

__ __   __ __   __ __ __
3 21   3 20   9 5 16

__ __   __ __ __ __ __ __
21 4   20 4 14 22 2 1

__ __ __ __ __ __ __.
15 25 20 21 2 19 25

3.
b. A BIG CAKE

c. I LIKE TO READ ABOUT DETECTIVES. IT IS FUN TO SOLVE A MYSTERY.

d. Codes are fun. Try to make up your own code. Write a message to someone, and ask him to write one back. Be sure to give him the key to your code.

4. a. A code is a kind of puzzle. Some codes are numbers, and some codes are letters. Another kind of code is called Morse code. It consists of dots and dashes. It was developed by Samuel Morse. Look at the copy of Morse code below.

Teacher's Note:
Morse Code may vary slightly. This is the International Morse Code.

A ._	M __	Y _.__
B _...	N _.	Z __..
C _._.	O ___	1 .____
D _..	P .__.	2 ..___
E .	Q __._	3 ...__
F .._.	R ._.	4 ...._
G __.	S ...	5 .....
H	T _	6 _....
I ..	U .._	7 __...
J .___	V ..._	8 ___..
K _._	W .__	9 ____.
L ._..	X _.._	0 _____

b. Try to decode the following message:

_   ....   .   _...   ..   __.   _._.   ._   ._.

__ __ __   __ __ __   __ __ __

..   ...   ._.   .   _..

__ __   __   __   __.

Do you think the code is easy to use? Morse code is often used to communicate with ships and airplanes. When it is used this way, it is tapped out as sounds over a telegraph-type wire.

4.
b. THE BIG CAR IS RED

c. Try to decode the following phrases:

_._.   ___   __   .   ___   ..._   .   ._.   _   __

__ __ __ __   __ __ __ __   __ __

__   _._   ....   ___   .._   ...   .

__ __   __ __ __ __ __ __.

c. COME OVER TO MY HOUSE

d. You have been introduced to spelling words in Lessons 29-32. Review these words.

5. a. Either orally or in writing, spell the following words for your teacher.

5. a. ✐ Teacher's Note: You may give sentences if your student needs it to understand the word given.

1)	coin	I have a *coin* for the gum machine.
2)	glue	I washed the sticky *glue* from my hands.
3)	learn	I will *learn* to play piano.
4)	noise	Did you hear that *noise*?
5)	current	The canoe tipped over in the swift *current*.
6)	difficult	Some things are easy; some things are *difficult*.
7)	flew	The bird *flew* away.
8)	field	The children play soccer in the *field*.

b. Listen to your teacher as she dictates sentences to you.

1) *I will eat a piece of bread with my soup.*

2) *Finally, he will hurry to be ready.*

b. ✐ Teacher's Note: Read the following sentences to your student to be written from dictation. Read slowly, repeating it several times. Encourage your student to just listen the first time, and then begin. Do not be concerned about saying it too often. The goal is for your student to be able to write the sentence. Speed and accuracy will be increased over time.

c. After your teacher has checked your sentence, make any corrections.

Cover your paper so that you can not see your corrected sentence. Listen again to your teacher as she dictates the same sentence again. Repeat the correction process.

c. ✐ Teacher's Note: After your student's first attempt, show him how to correct any mistakes. Read the sentence again, several times if needed. Repeat the correction process. Make sure to praise improvements. He may attempt it a third time if he desires; however, be alert to fatigue. If your student is overly tired or discouraged at this point, it is best to end the session, highlighting improvements.

d. Riddles are also puzzles that use words as their clues. When you read a riddle, you must think of the different ways words can be used. Here is an example:

I have wheels, but I often go for walks.
I carry someone special who someday will be able to push me around! What am I?

Did you guess it? The answer is a baby stroller. Riddles are little mysteries to which you are given clues.

e. 1) a clock
   2) a tree
   3) a pitcher

f. 1) a cloud
   2) an egg
   3) a football
   4) a table
   5) a shoe
   6) a balloon

e. Riddles can be about many different things. Here are some more riddles for you to solve:

1) I have a face and two hands, but I can not see. What am I?
2) I can be tall or small. I always have to stand. I have a lot of bark, but no bite! What am I?
3) I can hold water, or I can throw a baseball. What am I?

f. Here are some more riddles about things. See if you can guess what the answers are:

1) I am white and puffy. I am used to being up high. What am I?
2) I go up white and come down yellow. What am I?
3) You can throw me and catch me. You can kick me and hold me, but you can't roll me in a straight line. What am I?
4) I have legs, but I can't walk. I often have leaves. I am made of wood, but I am not a tree. What am I?
5) I often have a tongue, but I can't talk. Most people wouldn't leave home without me, though I do get kicked around a lot. What am I?
6) I can be skinny one minute and ready to pop the next. I go to all the best parties though people say I'm full of air. What am I?

g. Now, you try to write your own riddles. Riddles are usually three or four lines long. The first two or three lines are clues, and the last line is "What am I?" or "Who am I?" Pick something you see around you to start with. Read your riddle to your group and see if they get it. Don't worry if your first riddles seem too easy. You will think of more difficult riddles as you practice.

h. *Review Activities* are not needed for this lesson.

Randy

Robert

Rest

Run

Best

Boat

Bike

Back

Kind

Key

Know

Keep

Park

Plan

Pie

Put

EVERYDAY WORDS

New Skills	
Dictionary	Memorization
Encyclopedia	Oral Presentation

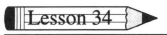

✐ **Teacher's Note:**
As your student completes each lesson, choose skills from the *Review Activities* that he needs. The *Review Activities* follow each lesson.

✐ **Teacher's Note:**
This week includes a trip to the library. If a library trip is not possible, you may use the encyclopedia.

See page 293.

See page 293.

See page 293.

 *Pledge of Allegiance*

I pledge allegiance to the flag, of the United States of America, and to the Republic for which it stands, one nation under God, indivisible, with liberty and justice for all.

1.   Listen as your teacher reads the literature passage. Write the poem from dictation the second time she reads it, or copy it. Compare your copy to the literature passage and make corrections.

2. a.   This is a statement that we can make as Americans. Many people in the world do not live in countries that express the beliefs we have in our Pledge of Allegiance.

   b.   Discuss with your teacher the proper way to say the Pledge o Allegiance - with your right hand over your heart, standing near an American flag, removing your hat if you are a boy or man.

   c.   If you have an American flag, practice saying the Pledge of Allegiance with your teacher. Since this pledge is often spoken in public, memorize it so you can join in with other Americans as it is said.

3. a.   There are many large, but important, words in our pledge. Read through the pledge with your teacher and make a list of words for which you do not know the meaning.

   b.   Look up these words in the dictionary and write them and their meanings.

   c.   After you have looked up unknown words, tell your teacher i your own words the meaning of the Pledge of Allegiance.

4. a.   Where did we get the Pledge of Allegiance and why do we say it? Look this up at the library. With your teacher's or librarian's assistance, look up "Pledge of Allegiance."

b. Using the filing system of the library, locate books that contain information on the pledge. If no other sources can be found, encyclopedias are very helpful. Discuss with your teacher or librarian how books are arranged in the library and how to locate the books you want.

c. Once you have found the books you want, write a paragraph of a few sentences on the Pledge of Allegiance. Indent the first sentence. Tell when it was written and by whom. Write about other information which you find interesting. Write down your information in complete sentences.

d. Ask your teacher for an American flag. Read your paragraph to a group, then lead them in properly saying the Pledge of Allegiance.

e. You are now going to review the spelling words presented in Lessons 1 - 15. Read over these spelling words.

Lesson 1	Lesson 2
knot	every
know	everybody
knee	everyone
knife	everything
knock	everywhere
BW - because	*BW* -Grandma

Lesson 3	Lesson 4
feel	pray
keep	crayon
wheel	holiday
seen	stay
need	gray
BW - really	*BW* - were

Lesson 7	Lesson 8
through	yellow
group	swallow
mouth	shadow
count	follow
ground	pillow
BW - always	*BW* - perhaps

4.

c. Although unverified, it is thought to have been written by Francis Bellamy or James B. Upham. It first appeared in a magazine, "Youth's Companion" in 1892.

✐ **Teacher's Note:**
If a flag is unavailable, a picture taped on the wall will be sufficient.

✐ **Teacher's Note:**
Orally test your student on a few words with which your student has had difficulty. Some students may be ready the same day to test, others may need a day or two. Any difficult words can be written on flashcards for your student's personal review.

Lesson 9
beach
treat
clean
peace
leave
BW - sincerely

Lesson 10
some
somebody
something
sometimes
somewhere
BW - night

Lesson 11
dirty
third
girl
bird
first
BW - along

Lesson 12
wear
year
clear
hear
dear
BW - queen

Lesson 13
sail
wait
plain
raise
hair
BW - tomorrow

Lesson 15
who
what
when
where
why
BW - reporter

f. Use a yellow highlighter pen (or a yellow crayon or colored pencil) to mark any words that seem hard to you. You may also want to ask your teacher which words you may have had trouble with before. Use your **SEE-SPELL-SAY** process to practice any words that give you trouble.

a. To prepare for your spelling test, use the *Student Activity Book* page provided. Or, fold your paper into quarters like this:

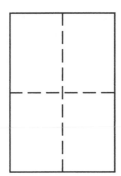

Then reopen the paper. Number your paper like this:

1.	11.
2.	12.
3.	13.
4.	14.
5.	15.
6.	16.
7.	17.
8.	18.
9.	19.
10.	20.

Read each word. Then read the sentence that uses the word, and read the word again.

1) group   I went to the park with a *group* of children.
2) third   She is in *third* grade.
3) beach   The *beach* has sand and water.
4) knock   Please *knock* on the door.
5) pillow   My favorite *pillow* is blue.
6) Grandma   *Grandma* is coming to visit.
7) wait   We must *wait* for the rain to stop.
8) year   On January first, it becomes the new *year*.
9) something Mom will give us *something* to do.
10) where   *Where* did your family go camping?
11) holiday   Christmas is a wonderful *holiday*.
12) please   *Please* help Mother clean up.
13) through   We can play when you are *through* doing your chores.
14) raise   He will *raise* the flag on the flagpole.
15) know   I *know* the answer.

✐ **Teacher's Note:**
If your student needs to focus on each section at a time so he will not feel overwhelmed, fold his paper so that he only sees one section.

See page 294.

16) first   Dad will set up the tent *first*.
17) follow   Will your dog *follow* you?
18) because   Mom called *because* it is time to go home.
19) were   We *were* going to the park.
20) everywhere   My dog goes *everywhere* with me.

Student Activity Book Page 343 - 345

Lake

Like

Look

Late

Lunch

The

Take

Fool

Turn

Trick

Fast

Food

Fun

Fix

Fence

Review Activities

1. *Alphabetical order*
   Write the words in each list in alphabetical order.

   a. party   balloon   candles   gifts

   b. flag   friend   fall   forest

   c. nation   navy   name   nail

1.
a. balloon
   candles
   gifts
   party

b. fall
   flag
   forest
   friend

c. nail
   name
   nation
   navy

267

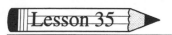
✐ **Teacher's Note:**
As your student completes each lesson, choose skills from the *Review Activities* that he needs. The *Review Activities* follow each lesson.

See page 294.

2.
b. Let's (let *us*) - children
you - children,
He - Jesus
(them) - children
them - children
them - children
His - God's

c. 1) He
2) her
3) They
4) We
5) It
6) her

"Jesus and the Children" *Scene II*
(Crowd of children pushing to try to see Jesus.)

John: *Let's stop pushing! Better still, why
don't you all go home? Jesus has had a
busy day. He is very tired and needs rest.
(All turn to go, some cry.)*

Jesus: *(Hearing them.) Do not send them
away! Let all the children come. God
wants them in His Kingdom the same as
grown-ups. (Children become quiet
and go toward Jesus.)*

Jesus, My Friend by Helen Kitchell Evans.
Used by permission of Shining Star
Publications, a Division of Good Apple, Inc.
Box 299 Carthage, Illinois 62321-0299

1.   Listen as your teacher reads the play. Copy the play.
Compare your copy to the play and make corrections.

                                           ★

2. a.   Words that take the place of nouns are called pronouns.
Here is a list of commonly used pronouns. Read them to
your teacher:

Pronouns								
I	me	you	he	she	they	me	his	mine
him	her	it	we	us	them	my		

   b.   Using this list, underline all the pronouns in our play, and tell
your teacher what noun each one replaced.

   c.   Use the correct pronoun to replace the italicized words.

     1) *John* is in bed. _____ is in bed.
     2) Please give it to *Sherry*. Please give it to _____.
     3) *Bob and Bill* are playing football. _____ are playing
        football.
     4) *Mother and I* like to cook. _____ like to cook.
     5) *The car* is green. _____ is green.
     6) The bag belongs to *Ann*. The bag belongs to _____.

d. Make up four sentences about family members. Use their names in each sentence, then rewrite each sentence, replacing the names with pronouns.

Ex: *Mother* and *Jeff* are going to church.
   They are going to church.

★

See page 285.

a. In Lesson 19, we talked about stage directions. Those are the directions in a play that tell the actors where to move and how to feel. There are parentheses ( ) around stage directions. These are not meant to be read or spoken out loud as a part of the play. Using a red pencil, underline the stage directions.

b. Using a blue pencil, underline only what the character named John says. Using a green pencil, underline only what Jesus says.

c. When we read something that is not a play, we know what someone has said or thought because their words are enclosed by quotation marks. Rewrite what John said by making it into a sentence with quotation marks. Begin by writing *John said*, followed by a comma. Put the first quotation mark before his actual words begin, and put the closing quotation mark after his last word and period. Remember to leave out stage directions.

d. Do the same thing with the words of Jesus. Begin by writing *Jesus said*, followed by a comma. Write his words as a sentence using quotation marks.

a. Listen as your teacher reads the Scripture that this play was taken from (Matthew 19:13-15). What do you think these children had to do to talk with Jesus? What if Jesus were in another town?

b. Did Jesus want to talk with the children? What does He do to show it? What can you do when you want to talk to Jesus? Do you think He wants to listen to you?

3.
a. (Crowd of children pushing to try to see Jesus.) (All turn to go, some cry.) (Hearing them.) (Children become quiet and go toward Jesus.)

b. John: Let's stop pushing! Better still, why don't you all go home? Jesus has had a busy day. He is very tired and needs rest. Jesus: Do not send them away! Let all the children come. God wants them in His Kingdom the same as grown-ups.

c. John said,"Let's stop pushing! Better still, why don't you all go home? Jesus has had a busy day. He is very tired and needs rest."

d. Jesus said, "Do not send them away! Let all the children come. God wants them in His kingdom the same as grown-ups."

4.
a. The children had to be in the same town, and be able to find Him while He was not busy.

b. Yes
He told John not to send them away.
Pray
Yes

c. Prayer is the way we can talk to Jesus anytime. When we come to Jesus in prayer, we need to be respectful - like the children in the play. Discuss with your teacher something you would like to bring to Jesus in prayer. Write a prayer to Him beginning with "Dear Jesus."

d. You are going to review the spelling words presented in Lessons 17-32. Read over these spelling words.

✎Teacher's Note: Orally test your student on a few words with which your student has had difficulty. Some students may be ready the same day to test, others may need a day or two. Any difficult words can be written on flashcards for your student's personal review.

Lesson 17
please
pleased
pleasing
grow
growing
BW - heavenly

Lesson 19
thought
bought
fought
ought
brought
BW - teacher

Lesson 20
wrong
write
wrap
wreck
wrote
BW - special

Lesson 24
right
bright
light
might
night
BW - wonderful

Lesson 25
morning
evening
sunrise
sunset
susnshine
BW -Sunday

Lesson 26
winter
summer
spring
garden
season
BW - fruit

Lesson 27
instead
head
dead
bread
ready
BW - pleasant

Lesson 29
noise
spoil
point
coin
boil
BW - difficult

Lesson 30   **Lesson 31**
new   chief
glue   believe
tool   field
soup   piece
flew   yield
BW - juice   *BW* - finally

Lesson 32
current
turn
early
learn
hurry
BW - victory

e. Use a yellow highlighter pen (or a yellow crayon or colored pencil) to mark any words that seem hard to you. You may also want to ask your teacher which words you may have had trouble with before. Use your **See-Spell-Say** process to practice any words that give you trouble.

a. To prepare for your spelling test, use *Student Activity Book*. Or, fold your paper into quarters, like this:

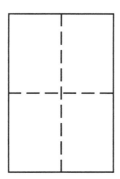

Then reopen the paper. Number your paper like this:

1.	11.
2.	12.
3.	13.
4.	14.
5.	15.
6.	16.
7.	17.
8.	18.
9.	19.
10.	20.

✐ **Teacher's Note:**
If your student needs to focus on each section at a time so he will not feel overwhelmed, fold his paper so that he only sees one section.

b. Read each word. Then read the sentence that uses the word, and read the word again.

1)	wrote	We *wrote* letters today.
2)	bright	The sun is very *bright* today.
3)	evening	It will be cooler in the *evening*.
4)	glue	We can fix the toy with some *glue*.
5)	bought	Dad *bought* a new fishing pole.
6)	point	That stick has a sharp *point*.
7)	early	It is too *early* to get up.
8)	believe	I *believe* his story.
9)	season	Summer is a wonderful *season*.
10)	ready	Mom and Dad are *ready* to go.
11)	noise	That car makes a lot of *noise*.
12)	please	*Please* wait for your sister.
13)	wrong	It is *wrong* to tell a lie.
14)	thought	Ann *thought* it was time to go.
15)	learn	I want to *learn* about boats.
16)	field	There are some flowers in the *field*.
17)	juice	Mom gave us some orange *juice*.
18)	instead	Come home now *instead* of later.
19)	garden	We planted vegetables in our *garden*.
20)	sunshine	The *sunshine* makes me feel warmer.

See page 294. ★

Jump

Jack

Jill

June

Ice

I'm

I'll

If

Dave

Date

Done

Did

Egg

Every

Eat

Eye

1.
a. We
b. He
c. His
d. It

2.
a. Tom said, "Emily is here."
b. "Come home soon," said Mom.
c. "I am so hungry," thought James.

Review Activities

Choose the skills your student needs to review.

1. *Pronouns*
   Replace the underlined words with pronouns.

   a. <u>Dad and I</u> went fishing.
   b. <u>Dad</u> caught four big fish.
   c. <u>Dad's</u> friend let us use the boat.
   d. <u>The trip</u> was fun.

2. *Quotation Marks*
   Add quotation marks to these sentences.

   a. Tom said, Emily is here.
   b. Come home soon, said Mom.
   c. I am so hungry, thought James.

A wise old owl sat in an oak.
The more he heard, the less he spoke;
The less he spoke, the more he heard.
Why aren't we all like that wise old bird?

Mother Goose Rhyme

Listen as your teacher reads the poem. Write the poem from dictation the second time she reads it, or copy it. Compare your copy to the literature passage and make corrections.

★ ──────────

a. Some verbs show past tense by adding **-ed**. Other verbs change their spelling to show that something has already happened. Underline the words in the literature passage that show past tense.

b. Point out each underlined word for your teacher and tell her the word which shows the action happening now (present tense).

Ex: slept - sleep

c. Match the following verbs with their irregular past tenses:

make	said
see	made
do	left
tell	saw
say	did
leave	told

d. Play Verb Tense Match-up.
Deal out seven cards to each player, and take turns drawing cards to make matches. The one with the most matches at the end wins.

a. There are some small words that come before nouns, and they tell us that a noun is coming. *A*, *an*, and *the* are called articles. Circle the words *a* and *an* in the literature passage. These words tell you that a noun is coming.

Continued on next page.

sit - sat
sing - sang
tell - told
keep - kept
hear - heard
have - had
say - said
take - took
speak - spoke
is - was
3.
b. 1) an
2) a

🖉 **Teacher's Note:**
Remind your student that
sometimes an article and
noun is separated by one
or more adjectives.
Ex: a big, shiny car

c. We use *a* **before a word**
that starts with a
consonant, and we use
an **before a word that**
starts with a vowel or
vowel sound. Ex: an
hour, an honorable deed

d. 1) an
2) a
3) a
4) an
5) An
6) a

See page 294.

4.
a. The owl learned to
speak less and listen
more.
b. Allow for discussion.
c. Allow for discussion.

See page 294.

b. Write the article which comes before *oak*.
1) _____oak

Write the article *a* or *an* which comes before *wise old owl*.
2) _____wise old owl

c. Look at this list and see if you can think of a rule that might tell you when to use *a* and when to use *an*:

an apple	a car	a bat
a dog	an egg	an umbrella

d. Write *a* or *an* in each blank:
1) I will get _____ice cream cone.
2) Bob and Jon are going on _____boat ride.
3) Dad will catch _____fish today.
4) Mom gave us _____orange for our snack.
5) _____animal ran out by the pond.
6) We will get _____dog for a pet.

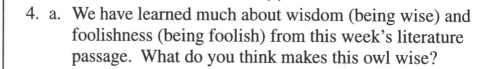

4. a. We have learned much about wisdom (being wise) and foolishness (being foolish) from this week's literature passage. What do you think makes this owl wise?

b. Discussing with your teacher, think of three wise things you have seen family members or friends do. Tell why you think what they did was wise. Why do you think they did it?

c. Since we are to learn from those who are wise, what did you learn from these three people?

d. If your teacher thinks it is a good idea, share with each of the three people what you thought about wise things they had done. Encouragement and appreciation are always gladly received.

5. If you have arrived at this activity, that means you have finished *The Yellow Book*. We are glad that you have used this book, and we would like to hear from you. Please write us a letter, and tell us what you liked the most about *The Yellow Book*. Please also tell us anything you did not like about it, so that we can keep making this a better book.

Here is our address:

The Yellow Book Authors (Debbie Strayer and Susan Simpson)
Common Sense Press
8786 Highway 21
Melrose, FL 32666

We look forward to hearing from students and teachers.

Safe

Some

Sweet

Sure

Side

Sleep

Great

Good

Girl

Game

Get

Grandma

Review Activities

Choose the skills your student needs to review.

1. *Irregular Verbs*
   Write the past tense of these verbs. Show that the action already happened.

   a. tell
   b. say
   c. leave
   d. do

2. *Articles*
   Write the article *a* or *an* in the blanks.

   a. _____ old goat
   b. _____ happy boy
   c. _____ snake
   d. _____ alligator

1.
a. told
b. said
c. left
d. did

2.
a. an
b. a
c. a
d. an

Assessment 8
(Lessons 34 - 36)

1. Add quotation marks to these sentences.

   a. May Sally come to the party asked Jane.
   b. Yes. She may come, replied Mom.
   c. Mom said you may ask Nancy also.
   d. Jane cried, we will have so much fun! I can hardly wait!

2. Replace the underlined words with pronouns.
   a. <u>Jason</u> likes baseball. _____ plays well.
   b. <u>Jason</u> is the best player on _____ team.
   c. <u>Mary</u> and I play piano. _____ like it.
   d. <u>Mary </u>has been playing since she was six years old. _____ is very good.

3. Write the past tense of these verbs. Show that the action already happened.
   a. see
   b. make
   c. leave
   d. tell

4. Write the articles *a* or *an* in the blanks.
   a. I need _____ drink of water.
   b. I will eat _____ apple.
   c. I saw _____ ape at the zoo.
   d. The cat chased ____ mouse.

1.
a. "May Sally come to the party?" asked Jane.
b. "Yes. She may come," replied Mom.
c. Mom said, "You may ask Nancy also."
d. Jane cried, "We will have so much fun!
   I can hardly wait!"

2.
a. He
b. his
c. We
d. She

3.
a. saw
b. made
c. left
d. told

4.
a. a
b. an
c. an
d. a

Enrichment Answers

The *Enrichment Activities* answers are listed below. Since the *Enrichment Activities* are not numbered, you can easily locate them by the Lesson number that proceeds it in the *Student Activity Book*. Some of the *Enrichment Activities* do not have a specific answer. For those, please read the directions in your student's book and evaluate the activity accordingly.

Lesson 1, 1b Word Search (Puzzle):
   knot   knee   know   knife   knock

Lesson 1, 5c
   Write the shortest word you know. (Answers will vary.)
   Write the longest word you know. (Answers will vary.)

Lesson 2, 1b Unscramble:
   1) eeryv   2) eeeewvryhr   3) eeeonrvy   4) eebdoyrvy   5) eegynrvhti
   1) every   2) everywhere   3) everyone   4) everybody   5) everything

Lesson 2, 5b Print Exercise:
   1) I sit on the chair and I <u>stand</u> on the floor.
   2) To finish something, I must first <u>start</u>.
   3) At night I can see the moon and the <u>stars</u>.
   4) I will sweep the floor with a <u>broom</u>.
   5) Be careful not to <u>break</u> the window.
   6) The dentist wants me to <u>brush</u> my teeth after every meal.

Lesson 3, 1b
   1) wheel   2) seen   3) keep   4) feel   5) need

Lesson 3, 2e Nouns:
   Answers will vary.
   1) The _____ flies.
   2) The _____ crawls.
   3) The _____ bounces.
   4) The _____ roars.
   5) The _____ speaks.
   6) The _____ cooks

Enrichment

Lesson 3, 5d

1) cup	A baby dog is called a <u>pup</u>.
2) hump	A gargage site is called a <u>dump</u>.
3) lake	Mom will <u>bake</u> some cookies.

Lesson 4, 1b (Puzzle)

pray   gray   crayon   holiday   stay

Lesson 4, 3d

1) There were pretty white <u>clouds</u> in the blue sky.
2) The teacher praised the students in her <u>class.</u>
3) I taught my dog some <u>tricks</u>.
4) Mom sat in the shade under the big <u>tree</u>.
5) Dad likes to fish for <u>trout</u>.

Lesson 4, 5e Letters in common:

1) i	2) g	3) e	4) n	5) y	6) o
simple	laugh	beep	chance	Billy	loose
drive	grow	forest	shin	Jenny	comb
fight	hinge	garden	only	Tommy	goat

Lesson 5, 1 Nouns

Answers will vary.

1) The _____ whistles.
2) The _____ sings.
3) The _____ plays.

4) The _____ barks.
5) The _____ hops.
6) The _____ shouts.

Lesson 5, 2b Matching:

1) oar -	2) fork -	3) spoon -	4) tennis ball -	5) pencil -
boat	plate of meat	bowl of soup	tennis racquet	paper

Lesson 5, 4d Pl and Dr:

1) Everybody should say <u>please</u> and thank you.
2) After I do my work, I can <u>play</u>.
3) I like peaches and <u>plums</u>.
4) My brother is learning how to <u>drive</u> a car.
5) Mom hangs out the clothes to <u>dry</u>.
6) My sister plays the piano, and I play the <u>drums</u>.

Lesson 7, 1b Unscramble:

1) count	2) mouth	3) group	4) through	5) ground
tonuc	mothu	gopur	roughth	roundg

Lesson 7, 3d Word that does not belong:

1) boy	2) city	3) planet	4) week	5) month	6) state
Sam	Rome	Saturn	Tuesday	February	California
boy	Paris	Mars	Thursday	month	Florida
Justin	city	Mercury	week	August	state
Ronnie	London	planet	Saturday	September	Michigan

Lesson 7, 4e Word that does not belong:

1) sad	2) tiny	3) bad	4) car	5) walk	6) sit
happy	big	pretty	arms	walk	run
glad	tiny	nice	car	smell	jog
sad	huge	pleasant	legs	taste	skip
joyful	large	bad	hands	hear	sit

Lesson 7, 5d Word that does not belong:

1) table	2) fork	3) destroy	4) f	5) joyful	6) grow
chair	fork	build	D	unhappy	branches
couch	cup	destroy	E	sad	grow
table	mug	make	f	gloomy	roots
sofa	glass	create	G	joyful	trunk

Lesson 8, 1b

1) yellow or pillow   2) swallow   3) pillow or yellow   4) shadow   5) follow

Lesson 8, 3e Word that does not belong:

1) sand	2) island	3) fly	4) bite	5) girl	6) bright
clams	island	fly	night	Susan	red
shrimp	ocean	pelican	light	girl	blue
oyster	lake	sparrows	bite	Tracy	purple
sand	river	crows	right	Sandy	bright

Lesson 8, 4e Word that does not belong:

1) run	2) eat	3) catch	4) bunny	5) throw	6) horse
run	milk	ocean	turtle	throw	small
shoes	eat	lake	lizard	nice	horse
sandals	juice	pool	bunny	kind	little
boots	tea	catch	snake	gentle	tiny

Lesson 9, 1b Fill in the blank with correct spelling word:
1) The opposite of dirty is <u>clean</u>.
2) We build a sandcastle on the <u>beach</u>.
3) The opposite of stay is <u>leave</u>.
4) *Greet* rhymes with <u>treat</u>.
5) The opposite of fighting is <u>peace</u>.

Lesson 9, 3e Put each word in its proper category:
1) Things you write with: pencil   marker   chalk
   Things you write on: notepad   paper   blackboard
2) Animals that fly: eagle   hawk   raven
   Animals that do not fly: mouse   rabbit   weasel
3) Things that move on water: rowboat   ship   sailboat
   Things that move on land: car   truck   bike

Lesson 9, 4e Put each word in its proper category:
1) Colors - red   blue   green
   Shapes - square   circle   triangle

2) Verbs, or doing words - hop   sit   yell
   Nouns, or naming words - frog   boy   girl

3) Things that move in the air - airplane   helicopter   rocket
   Things that move on land - car   truck   wagon

Lesson 9, 5b Put each word in its proper category:
1) Letters - D   G   H
   Numbers - 7   2   5

2) Baby animals - calf   foal   cub
   Adult animals - cow   horse   bear

3) Big animals - whale   elephant   giraffe
   Small animals - spider   butterfly   worm

Lesson 10, 1b Unscramble these spelling words:
1) something   2) somebody   3) somewhere   4) sometimes   5) some
meingthso   bdyoomes   hereoemsw   mmeessoti   meos

Lesson 10 - 3e Put each word in its proper category:
1) Days of the week - Tuesday Monday Saturday
   Months of the year - January March December

2) Words that begin with a small letter - girl boy friend
   Words that begin with a capital letter - James Sara Jack

3) Verbs - jump run grow
   Nouns - man dog tree

Lesson 10 - 4e How are words related? A=opposite B=same C=Word and doing word

1) A	2) A	3) C	4) C	5) C	6) B	7) B	8) C	9) B	10) B
big:	night:	Lion:	dog:	cow:	begin:	small:	pig:	shy:	over:
little	day	roar	bark	moo	start	tiny	oink	timid	above

Lesson 11 - 1b Spelling words: Fill in the blanks.
1) bird
2) girl
3) dirty
4) first
5) third

Lesson 11 - 3d Word relationships: A=opposite B=same C=word and doing word

1) B	2) A	3) C	4) B	5) A	6) A	7) B	8) A	9) C	10) C
end:	top:	bird:	close:	clean:	dry:	run:	hot:	horse:	monkey:
finish	bottom	fly	shut	dirty	wet	jog	cold	trots	climbs

Lesson 11 - 4c Word relationships:

1) B	2) B	3) C	4) A	5) A	6) A	7) B	8) C	9) C	10) A
quiet:	chop:	carpenter:	cool:	tall:	exit:	clever:	cat:	duck:	together:
silent	cut	builds	warm	rise	enter	smart	meows	quacks	apart

Lesson 11 - 5d

1) B	2) A	3) C	4) C	5) B	6) C	7) C	8) B	9) A	10) A
thin:	tall:	horn:	girl:	stiff:	baby:	rabbit:	bright:	dark:	strong:
slender	short	beeps	cooks	hard	sleeps	hops	colorful	light	weak

Lesson 12 - 1b
Find the word puzzle for: wear year clear hear dear

Lesson 12 - 3d Word relationships: A=opposite B=same C=word and doing word

1) C	2) C	3) B	4) B	5) B	6) A	7) C	8) B	9) B	10) B
hen:	rooster:	funny:	fix:	loud:	fast:	boys:	center:	grin:	breezy:
clucks	crows	humorous	mend	noisy	slow	play	middle	smile	windy

Lesson 12 - 4e Word relationships:

	1) B	2) B	3) B	4) A	5) A	6) C	7) C	8) B	9) B	10)
	fold:	under:	narrow:	yell:	sweet:	fish:	dolphin:	garbage:	tricky:	snak
	bend	beneath	thin	whisper	sour	swims	leaps	trash	cunning	slith

Lesson 12 - 5e Word relationships:

	1) C	2) C	3) B	4) A	5) A	6) B	7) A	8) A	9) A	10)
	student:	teacher:	ill:	near:	shiny:	look:	summer:	hot:	wild:	brid
	learns	teaches	sick	far	dull	see	winter	cold	tame	groo

Lesson 13 - 1b Fill in the blank with spelling words:
1) plain
2) wait or sail
3) raise
4) wait or sail
5) hair

Lesson 13 - 4e Word relationships: A=opposite B=same C=word and doing word

	1) A	2) A	3) B	4) C	5) C	6) B	7) A	8) B	9) C	10)
	high:	always:	glad:	eagle:	squirrel:	weary:	north:	rich:	deer:	east:
	low	never	happy	soars	chatters	tired	south	wealthy	prances	west

Lesson 13 - 5c Word relationships: A=whole: part B=sequence C=word and doing word

	1) A	2) A	3) C	4) C	5) C	6) C	7) B	8) B	9) B	10) A
	pig:	cat:	eyes:	tailor:	oven:	hammer:	first:	more:	January:	monk
	snout	claw	see	sews	bakes	pounds	second	most	February	tail

Lesson 15 - 1 b Spelling word puzzle:
who   what   when   where   why

Lesson 15 -3d Word relationships: A=whole: part B=sequence C=word and doing word

	1) A	2) C	3) B	4) A	5) C	6) B	7) A	8) B	9) C	10)
	wand:	tree:	morning:	arm:	fan:	day:	bike:	Monday:	ears:	7:8
	finger	grows	afternoon	elbow	blows	night	wheel	Tuesday	hear	

Lesson 15 - 4e See above.

	1) A	2) C	3) B	4) A	5) A	6) C	7) A	8) A	9) B	10) A
	foot:	bird:	first:	head:	word:	fish:	tree:	door:	9:10	book:
	toe	fly	second	ear	letter	swim	leaf	knob		page

Lesson 16 - 2c Word analogies:
1) hear   2) hands   3) neck   4) dog   5) hand   6) bird
eyes: see   socks: feet   sleeve: arm   claw: bird   nose: face   water: fish
ears: ___   gloves: ___   collar: ___   paw: ___   finger: ___   air: ___

Lesson 16 - 3c Word analogies:
1) dog   2) lamb   3) horse   4) sad   5) west   6) south
kitten: cat   bear: cub   calf: cow   laugh: happy   right: left   up: down
puppy: ___   sheep: ___   foal: ___   cry: ___   east: ___   north: ___

Lesson 16 - 4d Word analogies:
1) vegetable   2) pear   3) cold   4) chair   5) hear   6) dog
grapes: fruit   red: apple   stove: hot   sleep: bed   pictures: see   dog: cat
squash: ___   green: ___   refrigerator: ___   sit: ___   music: ___   cat: ___

Lesson 17 - 1b Unscramble spelling words:
1) pleased   2) grow   3) pleasing   4) growing   5) please
eealpds   orwg   easinglp   goingwr   eelpsa

Lesson 17 - 3d Word analogies:
1) cat   2) evening   3) cow   4) she   5) feet   6) winter
bark: dog   sunrise: sunset   eggs: hen   his: her   hat: head   swim: summer
purr: ___   morning: ___   milk: ___   he: ___   shoes: ___   ski: ___

Lesson 17 - 4d Word analogies:
1) m   2) u   3) B   4) H   5) should not   6) he will   7) I have
J: j   R: s   w: W   e: F   couldn't: could not   she'll: she will   they've: they have
M: ___   T: ___   b: ___   g: ___   shouldn't: ___   he'll: ___   I've: ___

Lesson 19 - 1b Fill in the blanks with spelling words:
1) brought   2) ought   3) thought   4) fought or bought   5) bought or fought

Lesson 19 - 2e Word analogies:
1) didn't   2) they'll   3) aren't   4) measure   5) mouse   6) no one
must not: musn't   we will: we'll   is not: isn't   pounds: weigh   children: child   everything: nothing
did not: ___   they will: ___   are not: ___   inch: ___   mice: ___   everyone: ___

Lesson 19 - 3e Word analogies:
1) noun   2) stopping   3) date   4) swim   5) tennis   6) read
run: verb   sit: sitting   clock: time   snow: ski   bat: baseball   pen: write
boy: ___   stop: ___   calendar: ___   water: ___   racquet: ___   book: ___

Lesson 19 - 4e Word analogies:

1) throw	2) hungry	3) grandfather	4) finish	5) unhappy	6) stop
kite: fly	drink: thirsty	bride: groom	begin: start	happy: glad	green: g
ball: ___	eat: ___	grandmother: ___	end: ___	sad: ___	red: __

Lesson 20 - 1b Word search spelling words:
wrong   wrap   write   wrote   wreck

Lesson 20 - 3e Word analogies:

1) sew	2) horn	3) milk	4) vegetable	5) apple	6) forest
wood: build	strum: guitar	coffee: tea	pie: dessert	yellow: lemon	cow: farm
cloth: ___	blow: ___	juice: ___	broccoli: ___	red: ___	racoon: __

Lesson 20 - 5e Word analogies:

1) 4	2) 3	3) twice	4) uncle	5) catch	6) double
first: 1	twins: 2	1: once	niece: nephew	pitcher: pitch	1: single
fourth: ___	triplets: ___	2: ___	aunt: ___	catcher: ___	2: ___

Lesson 21 - 1b

1) sweet	4) thin
2) swim	5) think
3) swans	6) thirty

Words that begin with <u>sw</u>:
1) The candy tastes _____.
2) I will learn to _____ in the pool.
3) There are ducks and _____ on the lake.
Words that begin with <u>th</u>:
4) My pencil is long and _____.
5) I must use my brain to _____.
6) Twenty and ten equal _____.

Lesson 21 - 2c Nouns:
Answers will vary.

1) The _____ hits.   4) The _____ swims.
2) The _____ runs.   5) The _____ dives.
3) The _____ yells.   6) The _____ splashes.

Lesson 21 - 4d Verbs:
Answers will vary.

1) A boy _____.   4) The lady _____.
2) A girl _____.   5) The man _____.
3) A man _____.   6) The baby _____.

Lesson 21 - 5b Change the first letter of the word on the left to fill in the sentence with the correct word:

1) crown	2) book	3) batter	4) pound	5) collar	6) rough
brown	cook	matter	found	dollar	tough

1) Many jewels were on the King's _____.   4) Mom bought a _____ of butter.
2) I will read my _____.   5) I put a tie on my _____.
3) Please mix the _____.   6) The carpenter sanded the ____wood

Lesson 22 - 1 Give directions:
1) right, down, left, up - clockwise around square
2) up, left, down, right - counter-clockwise around square

Lesson 22 - 2d Write the word that comes next:
1) dinner   2) third   3) spring   4) night or evening   5) March
6) adult or grown-up
    1) breakfast, lunch, _____.   4) morning, noon, _____.
    2) first, second, _____.   5) January, February, _____.
    3) fall, winter, _____.   6) baby, teenager, _____.

Lesson 22 - 5c Give directions:
1) north, east, south, west - clockwise around square
2) south, east, north, west - counter-clockwise around square

Lesson 24 - 1b Fill in the blanks with words spelling words:
1) right   2) bright   3) night   4) might   5) light

Lesson 24 - 3c Fill in the blanks with words beginning with ch and cr:
1) checkers   4) crab   1) I like to play chess and _____.
2) chat   5) crack   2) A little talk is called a _____.
3) choose   6) crumbs   3) I will _____ the red one or the blue one.
    4) The men fish for lobsters and _____.
    5) Dad will fix the _____ on the window.
    6) The ants ate the _____ after the picnic.

Lesson 24 - 4d Write the word that comes next:
1) yard   2) run   3) hot   4) large   5) lightest   6) heaviest
    1) inch, foot, _____.   4) small, medium, _____.
    2) walk, jog, _____.   5) light, lighter, _____.
    3) cold, warm, _____.   6) heavy, heavier, _____.

Lesson 24 - 5e Circle the word that does not rhyme:
1) long 2) mink 3) stock 4) mat 5) kit 6) truck 7) sail 8) mark 9) long
    1) sing, thing, bring, long   6) lake, truck, sake, bake
    2) trunk, dunk, mink, sunk   7) pile, while, sail, tile
    3) crack, stack, stock, back   8) star, jar, car, mark
    4) sit, bit, slit, mat   9) long, small, ball, call
    5) sick, kit, lick, tick

Lesson 25 - 1b Unscramble spelling words:

1) sunset   2) morning   3) evening   4) sunrise   5) sunshine
   sstenu   ringnom   vingeen   isunsre   ssnnieuh

Lesson 25 - 3e Words that begin with <u>wr</u> and <u>gr</u>:

1) write   4) grass   1) I will _____ a letter.
2) wrong   5) grateful   2) He was right, and I was _____.
3) wrap   6) grapes   3) I will _____ the gift with shiny paper.
                                           4) Dad mows the _____.
                                           5) If you are thankful, you are _____.
                                           6) _____ are one of my favorite fruits.

Lesson 25 - 4d Nouns:

Answers will vary.   1) The _____ plays.   4) The _____ gallops.
                               2) The _____ works.   5) The _____ chirps.
                               3) The _____ listens.   6) A _____ buzzes.

Lesson 25 - 5b Verbs: 1) My brother _____.   4) My friend _____.
Answers will vary.   2) My sister _____.   5) My neighbor _____.
                                      3) My father _____.   6) My mother _____.

Lesson 26 - 1b Fill in the blanks with spelling words:

1) summer   2) spring   3) season   4) winter   5) garden
1) We swim in the _____.   4) I wear a coat in the _____.
2) The flowers bloom in the _____.   5) In the spring we plant our _____.
3) Spring is may favorite _____.

Lesson 26 -2e Words that begin with <u>kn</u>, <u>fl</u>, <u>qu</u>:   1) I will tie a _____.
1) knot   4) flew   7) queen   2) My sister likes to sew and _____
2) knit   5) flat   8) quart   3) I hear a _____ on the door.
3) knock   6) flipper   9) quick   4) The bird _____ away.
                                                        5) The land has no hills, it is _____
                                                        6) The dolphin waved his _____.
                                                        7) The king and _____ sat on the thron
                                                        8) Two pints equal one _____.
                                                        9) A turtle is slow, and a rabbit is ____

Lesson 26 - 4e Write an adjective for each noun:

Answers will vary.   1) _____ flower   4) _____ boy   7) _____ house
                               2) _____ fish   5) _____ girl   8) _____ boat
                               3) _____ luncheon 6)_____ man   9) _____ tree

Lesson 27 - 1b Fill in the blanks with spelling words:
   1) dead or head   2) bread   3) ready   4) instead   5) head or dead

Lesson 27 - 2d Questions about diagram: _____
   1) DEFGH 2) FGH 3) ABCDE 4) ABC 5) DE 6) IJ
   1) What letters are in the square? 2) Only in the square?
   3) In the circle?   4) Only in the circle?
   5) Both circle and square?   6) Outside circle and square?

Lesson 27 - 3c On a separate sheet of paper, write your name, allowing a column for each
        letter of your name. Underneath each letter, think of as many foods as you
        can that begin with that letter.
  Answers will vary.

Lesson 27 - 5d Each word represents a whole. List three things that are a part of the whole.
  Possible answers may include:
  insect   1)   head, legs, thorax, antenna
  door   2)   hinge, wood, knob
  computer 3)   drives, keyboard, monitor
  mouse   4)   head, tail, body, feet, whiskers
  house   5)   roof, sides, porch, rooms
  family   6)   parents, sister, brother, grandma

Lesson 28 - 1 Think of things you can put in a suitcase that begin with the letters in suitcase.
  Answers will vary.

Lesson 28 - 4b Fill in the blanks with words beginning with pr and bl.
  1) prays   4) blink   1) The church _____ for the sick.
  2) pricked   5) blocks   2) The needle _____ my finger.
  3) price   6) black   3) The _____ was $2.00.
                              4) I will keep my eyes open and not _____.
                              5) The baby plays with her building _____.
                              6) The old photograph was in _____ and white.

Lesson 28 - 5c Write an adjective for each noun:
  Answers will vary.   1) _____ mountain   4) _____ rain
                          2) _____ sunset   5) _____snow
                          3) _____ rainbow   6) _____clouds

Lesson 29 - 1b Fill in the blanks with spelling words:
   1) boil   2) point   3) spoil   4) noise   5) coin

Lesson 29 - 5c Josh is taller than Mike. Mike is taller than Steve.
Label the pictures of the boys.

Josh   Steve   Mike

Lesson 30 - 1b Word search - spelling words:
  new glue flew tool soup

Lesson 30 - 4e Jill is shorter than Lizzie. Kuzzue is shorter than Amy. Label the pictures of th
     girls.

Amy   Lizzie   Jill

Lesson 30 - 5e Circle the word that does not rhyme.
  1) tear 2) back 3) gas 4) chin 5) with 6) cork 7) flock 8) tick 9) rip

  1) tear, oar, core, soar   6) corn, born, torn, cork
  2) king, back, wing, thing   7) flock, home, dome, foam
  3) jog, log, cog, gas   8) sock, rock, clock, tick
  4) chew, chin, flew, clue   9) rip, hot, not, pot
  5) with, write, kite, flight

Lesson 31 - 1b Fill in the blanks with spelling words.
  field   yield   believe   piece   chief

Lesson 31 - 2d Words beginning with fr and gl:
  1) from   4) glass   1) This is to you, _____ me.
  2) friend   5) glad   2) Josh is my best _____.
  3) fresh   6) glitter, glow 3) We eat _____vegetables from our garde
                                 4) I will pour a _____ of milk.
                                 5) I am not sad; I am _____.
                                 6) The stars sparkle and _____.

Lesson 31 - 4e Verbs:
  Answers will vary.   1) The dog _____.   4) The carpenter _____.
                         2) The cat _____.   5) The mother _____.
                         3) The mouse _____. 6) The student _____.

Lesson 31 - 5e Fill in the word that comes next:
1) smallest   2) quickest   3) loudest   4) most   5) always   6) darkest
small, smaller, quick, quicker, loud, louder, few, more, never, sometimes, dark, darker,

Lesson 32 - 1b Word search - spelling words:
current   early   hurry   turn   learn

Lesson 32 - 3e Write an adjective describing each noun:
Answers will vary.   1) _____ mice   3) _____ monkeys   5) _____ floor
                      2) _____ horses 4) _____ day   6) _____ room

Lesson 32 - 4e Diagram:
1) S   4) 2
2) X   5) 4
3) S   6) 3

| A B C D E F G |
| H I J K L M N |
| O P Q R S T U |
| V W X Y Z 1 2 |

1) Start at D, go down 2, go right 1.
2) Start at M, go left 3, go down 2.
3) Start at G, go left 2, go down 2.
Where are you?

Lesson 34 - 1 Write at least one grocery item for each letter of the word G R O C E R I E S
possible answers:
g - gum, grapes
r - radishes
o - onions, olives
c - celery, cherries
e - eggs
r - relish
i - ice cream
e - eggplant
s - sunflower seeds

Lesson 34 - 2c Adjectives describing nouns:
Answers will vary.   1) _____ fire   3) _____moon   5) _____ shoe
                      2) _____star   4) _____ hat   6) _____jacket

Lesson 34 - 3c Write as many words as you can using letters from the word ENCYCLOPEDIA.
Answers will vary.

Lesson 34 - 5a
slide   sit   read   jump

cry   sing   ride   shout

Lesson 35 - 1 Write as many words as you can using the letters in the word WASHINGT(
    Answers will vary.

Lesson 35 - 2d Using a clock or watch, write down how long it takes to:
    Answers will vary.   1) Count from 1 to 100.
                              2) Flip a coin and get heads ten times.
                              3) Hop on one foot with your arms held in front of y
                              4) Say the alphabet.
                              5) Count from 100 backwords to 1.

Lesson 35 - 5a Discussion with teacher: Circle the correct answer.
    1) toy   2) needle and thread   3) stamp   4) bandage   5) ladder
    6) hot   7) careful   8) animal   9) bed   10) something to wear

    1) A penpal is visiting you from another country. He says to you,
       "Let's play. I will get a **thlimper**."
       Do you think **thlimper** is a kind of toy, a number, or something to eat?
    2) "I will teach you how to sew. Do you have a **koomp and klump**?"
       Do you think **koomp and klump** is bacon and eggs, bat and ball, or needle and
       thread?
    3) "I want to mail this letter. I need a **zimfer**."
       Do you think a **zimfer** is a zipper, button, or stamp?
    4) "I cut my finger. Do you have a **dunker**?"
       Do you think a **dunker** is a pen, donut, or bandage?
    5) "We can't reach the apples. Let's get a **flump**."
       Do you think a **flump** is a flashlight, ladder, or cup?
    6) "The sun has been shining all day. I am so **shlomp**."
       Do you think **shlomp** means hungry, hot, or worried?
    7) "The stairs are broken. Be **poshle**!"
       Do you think **poshle** means happy, careful, or late?
    8) "The hairy **fungu** crawled into the bushes."
       Do you think **fungu** is a type of ball, an animal, or something to eat?
    9) "I am very tired. Where is a **shlacky**?"
       Do you think **shlacky** is a type of game, an animal, or a bed?
    10) "i need a **zoogla**. It is raining."
       Do you think **zoogla** is something to eat, an animal, or something to wear?

Lesson 36 - 1 Analogies:

1) block
2) gobble
3) patient
4) he
5) they
6) his
7) elephant
8) foot
9) arm
10) more
11) heard
12) sat
13) wise
14) green
15) pink

1) round: bell: : square: _____
2) duck: quack: : turkey: _____
3) teacher: student: : doctor: _____
4) Jennifer: she: : Tommy: _____
5) Jim and I: we: : Jim and Tom: _____
6) Kim's: hers: : Tom's: _____
7) snout: pig: : trunk: _____
8) thumb: hand: : toe: _____

9) knee: leg: : elbow: _____
10) least: most: : less: _____
11) see: saw: : hear: _____
12) stand: stood: : sit: _____
13) tall: short: : foolilsh: _____
14) blue and red: purple: :
    yellow and blue: _____
15) white and black: gray: :
    white and red: _____

Lesson 36 - 3d

1) Sara Jill Tracy
2) Brandi Katy Jessica
3) Kim

1) Jill is older than Sara, but younger than Traci. List the children in order from youngest to oldest.
2) Kay is shorter than Jessica. Brandi is shorter than Katy. List the children in order from shortest to tallest.
3) Kim is faster than Ashley. Ashley is faster than Emily. Emily is faster than Tonya. Who is the fastest girl?

Lesson 36 - 4d

Answers will vary.
1) List the words you might hear on a fishing trip.
2) List the words you might hear while fixing dinner at home.

Skills Index

The numbers listed after each skill refer to the Lesson numbers.

Composition

Creative Expression and Games

Grammar

Higher Order Thinking Skills

Memorization - 11,13,24,25,26,27,34
Alphabetical order - 5,7,28
Charts and graphs - 17
Cause and effect - 3

Reading

Cause and effect - 3
Characters - 19
Compare and contrast - 14
Comprehension - 6,9,14,18
Fiction and nonfiction - 32
Indent - 6,7
Legend - 18
Lines - 19
Main idea - 6
Paragraph - 6,10

Plays - 19,35
Predicting outcome - 32
-ed - 21
-igh - 4
-le - 7,12
-ng - 10
-tion - 15
Syllable - 7,11,12,13,26
Vocabulary - 3,6,14,18,21,23,25,29

Spelling

ea - 9,12,17,27
ee - 3
er, ar, or - 31
ie - 31
igh - 10,24
kn - 1
ay - 4

le, el, al - 30
oi - 29
ur, ear - 32
wr - 20
ou - 7
ow - 8,17
ir - 11

ai - 13
wh - 15
ough - 19
oo - 30
ue - 30
ew - 30

Study Skills

Alphabetical order - 5,7,28
Bar graph - 17
Charts - 17
Compare and contrast - 14, 23,30,31
Compass - 16
Dictionary - 11,18,21,23,24,29,33,34
Directions - 9,16
Encyclopedia - 12,23,30,34
Fact and opinion - 22

Graphs - 17
Map skills - 14,16
Memorization - 11,13,24,25,26,27,34
Newspaper - 15
Phone book - 5,28
Research - 34
Sequencing - 27
Tally marks - 17
Thesaurus - 2,8,27
Timeline - 23

Optional Books Used in the Literature Links

Bemelman, Ludwig. *Madeline*. Penguin Group.

Dalgliesh, Alice. *The Courage of Sarah Noble*. Simon & Schuster.

Heilbroner, Joan. *Meet George Washington*. Random House.

Shub, Elizabeth. *The White Stallion*. Random House.